D1142532

The Bible in Human Transformation

FACETS

Selected Titles in the Facets Series

The Bible in Human Transformation

*Toward a New Paradigm
for Biblical Study*

Walter Wink

Fortress Press
Minneapolis

THE BIBLE IN HUMAN TRANSFORMATION
Toward a New Paradigm for Biblical Study

Copyright © 2010 Fortress Press, an imprint of Augsburg Fortress. All rights reserved. Except for brief quotations in critical articles or reviews, no part of this book may be reproduced in any manner without prior written permission from the publisher. Visit http://www.augsburgfortress. org/copyrights/or write to Permissions, Augsburg Fortress, Box 1209, Minneapolis, MN 55440.

Library of Congress Cataloging-in-Publication data
Wink, Walter.
   The Bible in human transformation : toward a new paradigm for biblical study / Walter Wink.
       p. cm.
   Originally published: Philadelphia : Fortress Press, 1973.
   ISBN 978-0-8006-9633-7 (alk. paper)
   1.   Bible—Study and teaching. 2.   Bible—Criticism, interpretation, etc.—History. I. Title.
   BS600.3.W57 2010
   220.07—dc22

                                        2009042000

The paper used in this publication meets the minimum requirements of American National Standard for Information Sciences—Permanence of Paper for Printed Library Materials, ANSI Z329.48–1984.

Manufactured in the U.S.A.

14   13   12   11   10   1   2   3   4   5   6   7   8   9   10

Contents

Preface to the 2010 Edition

Almost four decades have passed since *The Bible in Human Transformation* was first published. What originally drove the book was my desire to change the way people engaged in Bible study in order to bring about transformation in their lives. I think I have been at least somewhat successful in that goal. I have been gratified by the many expressions of appreciation for the approach I take here. I am also heartened by the polemical responses of critics, since these responses demonstrate that they have paid sincere attention to my concerns!

I can honestly say that my desire to enliven Bible reading has not changed in the intervening decades. What *has* changed is that in these decades I have personally experienced the oppression of peoples in South Africa and Chile under dictatorships and have known those who have struggled with poverty and suffering. If anything, these experiences have intensified my desire to open the good news of the Bible to bring freedom and hope to the world. As a result I have concentrated my writing on the encounter between the nonviolent teaching of Jesus and the Powers That Be. This has meant that I deal not only with political issues but also, for example, with the way that social attitudes toward homosexuality amount to psychic "Powers That Be." All of these endeavors are in the interest of freeing human beings from bondage.

Many others have shared this goal of enlarging freedom for all. What I have come to see is that Jesus' teaching was not just that we should be free, but that we should be *human.* Oppression, poverty, and suffering inhibit our freedom to move on to the real point of the gospel: to become fully human beings.

As I look around now, I have been gratified by how many pastors, youth workers, and educators are using the

new paradigm that I propose here. I am concerned, however, that this approach to understanding the message of
Jesus might become just one more way to study the Bible
rather than what I hope will be a genuine paradigm shift.
In the first edition I wrote that I wanted to turn my back
on the modernist-fundamentalist debate, but that debate
continues to distract us from our human quest.

My purpose here is not so much to interact with past
responses to the book as to invite the reader to consider anew my plea in these pages for a different way of
approaching the Bible. My hope, at the beginning of the
twenty-first century, is that the republication of this book
will help the reader respond to the questions I posed not
only in *The Bible in Human Transformation* but also in my
later work, *The Human Being*: Before he was worshiped as
God incarnate, how did Jesus struggle to incarnate God?
Before he became identified as the source of all healing,
how did he relate to, and how did he teach his disciples
to relate to, the Source of all healing? Before forgiveness
came to be understood solely as a function of his cross, how
did Jesus understand people to have been forgiven? Before
the kingdom of God became a compensatory afterlife or a
future utopia adorned with all the political trappings that
Jesus resolutely rejected, what did he mean when he pro-
claimed the nearness of "the kingdom"? Before he became
identified as Messiah, how did he relate to the profound
meaning of the messianic image? Before he himself was
made the sole mediator between God and humanity, how
did Jesus experience and communicate the presence of
God? (See *The Human Being: Jesus and the Enigma of the
Son of Man* [Minneapolis: Fortress, 2002], p. 2.)

I wish to thank my friend Dr. Thomas Michael, Profes-
sor Emeritus in the Department of Management of Rowan
University in Glassboro, New Jersey, for help in writing this
preface. I am grateful for all those who have sustained me
through a difficult illness. I look forward to you, the reader,
joining me in working through these questions.

Preface

This essay springs from a particular context which at one and the same time limits its general applicability and gives it whatever relevance it may possess. It is directed to the American theological scene and is written by a white male in a liberal Protestant seminary. It belongs to a chorus of voices raised in the name of God and humanity against a form of scholarship gone to seed but which, by sheer abundance of seeds, flourishes everywhere in this land. I count myself as ally in this outcry with James Smart and James M. Robinson, Paul Minear and Amos Wilder, Robert Funk and Brevard Childs, to name but a few. But I have had to go my own way.

I originally conceived this essay as a tract. But alas, since no one wants to publish tracts today, I was left with the option of suiting the publishing business and adding a few pages. In fact I didn't add enough. Most readers have challenged me to do a sequel spelling out with case studies the process which I all too briefly have described here, a challenge which I am only too eager to accept. What I have written is more programmatic than program, more manifesto than manifest, but I believe it is moving in the right direction: toward a mode of Bible study which facilitates transformation in human lives.

Throughout the essay I have assumed the victory of the critical consciousness, even though vast reserves of precritical mentality remain on our continent. I am especially concerned that these arguments not be seized upon by reactionary dogmatists and used against those who still struggle for freedom of inquiry and an empirical method. We are all gasping for air in the space we are given. But if, as I believe, the terms of the modernist-fundamentalist debate were mistaken from the start, it is I hope not irresponsible to turn my back on that conflict and try to take a step in a different direction.

I have greatly benefited from the astringent criticisms and buoying encouragement of my colleagues at Union Theological Seminary: Henry Mottu, David Lotz, J. Louis Martyn, Tom Driver, Beverly Harrison, Cyril C. Richardson, George Landes, James Bergland, Robert E. Neale, William A. Simpson. Special thanks are due to Elizabeth B. Howes and Sheila Moon, analysts in the Jungian tradition, for their perceptive comments on the manuscript, and for the opportunity to spend a sabbatical leave working under their supervision in the Guild for Psychological Studies in San Francisco; and to Union Seminary and the American Association of Theological Schools for making the leave possible.

–Walter Wink

*It is terrible to die of thirst in
the ocean. Do you have to salt your
truth so heavily that it does not
quench thirst any more?*
—Nietzsche

1

The Bankruptcy of
the Biblical Critical Paradigm

Historical biblical criticism is bankrupt.

I use "bankrupt" in the exact sense of the term. A business which goes bankrupt is not valueless, nor incapable of producing useful products. It still has an inventory of expensive parts, a large capital outlay, a team of trained personnel, a certain reputation, and usually, until the day bankruptcy is declared, a façade which appeared to most to be relatively healthy. The one thing wrong—and the only thing—is that it is no longer able to accomplish its avowed purpose for existence: to make money.

It is in this precise sense that one can speak of the historical critical method generally, and of its application to biblical studies in particular, as bankrupt. Biblical criticism has produced an inventory of thousands of studies on every question which has seemed amenable to its methods, with a host of additional possibilities still before it. It has a method which has proven itself in earlier historical periods to be capable of remarkable achievements. It has in its employ hundreds of competent, trained technicians. Biblical criticism is not bankrupt because it has run out of things to say or new ground to explore. It is bankrupt solely because it is incapable of achieving what most of its practitioners considered its purpose to be: so to interpret the Scriptures that the past becomes alive and illumines our present with new possibilities for personal and social transformation.

How did biblical criticism become insolvent? Here are at least a few of the reasons.

1. The method as practiced was incommensurate with the intention of the texts.

The writers of the New Testament bore witness to events which had led them to faith. They wrote "from faith to faith," to evoke or augment faith in their readers. Ostensibly, historical criticism is not hostile to these intentions, but should serve to make the same decision for faith or unfaith accessible across the gulf of centuries to readers today. In actual practice, however, this seldom happens, and for good reason. For the very essence of scientific and historical inquiry in modern times has been the suspension of evaluative judgments and participational involvement in the "object" of research. Such detached neutrality in matters of faith is not neutrality at all, but already a decision against responding. At the outset, questions of truth and meaning have been excluded, since they can only be answered participatively, in terms of a lived response. Insofar as they are retained at all, "truth" is reduced to facticity, and the test's "meaning" is rendered by a paraphrase.

Such "objective neutrality" thus requires a sacrifice of the very questions the Bible seeks to answer. But if our questions do not anticipate a certain type of answer, how can we hope to receive it? If our methodology is not designed to reveal meaning, the possibility that meaning might emerge is blocked in advance, through the manner in which the problem is stated. Having initially turned to the text seeking insights about living, we find ourselves ineluctably drawn by our method further and further from the place where the text might speak.

This detached, value-neutral, ahistorical point of view is, of course, an illusion. For all empirical work can be carried out only on the basis of certain meta-empirical, ontological, and metaphysical judgments, and the expectations and hypotheses which follow from them. "He who makes no decisions has no questions to raise and is not even able to formulate a tentative hypothesis which enables him to set a problem and to search history for its answer."[1]

Historical criticism did operate, although covertly, on the basis of such meta-empirical underpinnings: a faith in reason and progress and an ontology of naïve realism. In the context of belief in progress, historical method became the means to delineate the development of ideas and institutions toward that historical apex *modern times*. It is clear in all this that the "objective standpoint" is none other than the historically conditioned place where *we* happen to be standing, and possesses no neutrality or detachment at all.

We will see later that the historical critical method had a vested interest in undermining the Bible's authority, that it operated as a background ideology for the demystification of religious tradition, that it required functional atheism for its practice, and that its attempted mastery of the object was operationally analogous to the myth of Satan and the legend of Faust. For the time being the point is solely that the fiction of "detachment" made vital relatedness to the content of the text impossible. By detaching the text from the stream of my existence, biblical criticism has hurled it into the abyss of an objectified past. Such a past is an infinite regress. No amount of devoted study can bring it back.

The biblical writers themselves never treated their own past in such a manner. Their past was a continual accosting, a question flung in their paths, a challenge, and a confrontation. But because the scholar has removed himself from view, no shadow from the past can fall across his path. He has insulated himself from the Bible's own concerns. He examines the Bible, but he himself is not examined—except by his colleagues in the guild! This disregard of the voices of the past, this systematic stopping of the ears and restraint of the will do not constitute objectivity but are instead the negation of the manifest intent of the subject matter.

The historical critical method has reduced the Bible to a dead letter. Our obeisance to technique has left the Bible sterile and ourselves empty. The further we have advanced in analysis the more the goal has receded from our sight, so that today many of us might well say with Nietzsche, *"Ich habe meine Gründe vergessen"*—I have forgotten why I ever began.[2]

2. The ideology of objectivism drew historical criticism into a false consciousness.

Objectivism as used here refers to the academic ideal of detached observation of phenomena without interference by emotions, will, interests, or bias. It can be spoken of as an ideology because it does not correspond to reality and is incapable of realization. The error of objectivism as an ideology lies in its intellectualism, its blindness to the irrational or unconscious, and its separation of theory from practice. Its falsehood lies in the systematic repression of its error.

Objectivism is intellectualistic. Intellectualism, says Mannheim, is "a mode of thought which either does not see the elements in life and in thought which are based on will, interest, emotion, and *Weltanschauung*—or, if it does recognize their existence, treats them as though they were equivalent to the intellect and believes that they may be mastered by and subordinated to reason."[3] Intellectualism is characterized by a complete separation of theory from practice, of intellect from emotion, and finds emotionally determined thinking intolerable. When it encounters a mode of thinking which is necessarily set in an irrational context, as political or religious thought always is, the attempt is made so to construe the phenomena that the evaluative elements will appear separable from a residue of pure theory. Left obscured is the question of whether in fact the emotional is so intertwined with the rational as to involve even the categorical structure itself, thus making the sought-for isolation of the evaluative elements *de facto* impossible.[4]

Here the problem of the academy becomes unavoidable, with its endemic separation of theory from practice, mind from body, reason from emotion, knowledge from experience. Is anything but intellectualism possible when our questions do not arise primarily out of the struggle with concrete problems of life and society, from the blistering exposure to trial and error, from the need for wisdom in the ambiguous mash of events? Can historical criticism, practiced in the academy, ensnared in an objectivist ideology, ever do more than simply refer the data of the text away from an encounter with experience and back to its own uncontrolled premises?

In such a context biblical study is rendered innocuous from the start. Here we are trained to think in a framework which strives to negate every evaluation, every trace of mundane meaning, every proclivity toward a view of the whole. The result is a hermeneutic with whose categories not even the simplest life-process can be thought through. The outcome of biblical studies in the academy is a trained incapacity to deal with the real problems of actual living persons in their daily lives.

Objectivism is not simply in error, however. It is a false consciousness. Error is unintentional. Falsehood knows but has sought to forget its own face. Objectivism is a false consciousness because evidence of its error is systematically repressed. It pretends detachment when in fact the scholar is attached to an institution with a high stake in the socialization of students and the preservation of society, and when he himself has a high stake in advancement in that institution by publication of his researches. It pretends to be unbiased when in fact the methodology carries with it a heavy rationalistic weight which by inner necessity tends toward the reduction of irrational, subjective, or emotional data to insignificance or invisibility. It pretends to search for "assured results," "objective knowledge," when in fact the method presumes radical epistemological doubt, which by definition devours each new spawn of "assured results" as a guppy swallows her children. It pretends to suspend evaluations, which is simply impossible, since research proceeds on the basis of questions asked and a ranked priority in their asking. But such judgments presuppose a system of values and an ontology of meanings which not only give weight to the questions but make it possible to ask them at all. Even the choice of syntax and vocabulary is a political act that defines and circumscribes the way "facts" are to be experienced—indeed, in a sense even creates the facts that can be studied.[5] And finally, objectivism pretends to be neutral when in fact the scholar, like everyone else, has racial, sexual, and class interests to which he is largely blind and which are unconsciously reflected in his work. (Why, for example, do German scholars persist in using the offensive term "*Spätjudentum*," as if Judaism ceased to exist with the rise of Christianity? Why are there so few women and Black biblical scholars in this country? Why has hermeneutical scholarship so long ignored the rich tradition of Black preaching?)

On the American scene the problem has been exacerbated by the struggle to gain standing for departments of religious studies in secular universities previously closed to all religious instruction. In order to dissociate religious studies from denominational and dogmatic stigmatization, it seemed necessary to assert the scientific character of the discipline. The descriptive approach became the magic key to academic respectability. This has in actual practice meant objectivism with a vengeance, and accounts at least in part for the virtual abandonment recently (regardless of theoretical leanings, which were often of the best sort) of the beachhead which Bultmann had established.

Objectivity is much to be desired. But objectivity must be separated off from the ideology of objecti*vism* and given new footing. A new type of objectivity is attainable, not through the exclusion of evaluations, but through the critical awareness and proper use of them. Lest this be construed as counsel simply to try harder under the old presuppositions, let us be clear that what is demanded in the face of bankruptcy is not a pep talk to the sales force but new management. If all historical knowledge is relational knowledge, and can only be formulated with reference to the position of the observer, we are faced with the task of developing a radically different model for the role of the interpreter vis-à-vis the text.

3. Biblical studies increasingly fell prey to a form of technologism which regards as legitimate only those questions which its methods can answer.

Technique is absolutely essential in any field of inquiry. But technique is essentially value-blind. It depends for its functioning on orders given outside its area of competence. It is all the more crucial then that the technique employed be commensurate with its object, for techniques can only produce those results for which they are created. I have already argued above that the historical method as practiced has not been adequately commensurate with the biblical texts. In this case the carrying over of methods from the natural sciences has led to a situation where we no longer ask what we would like to know and what will be of decisive significance for the next step in personal or social development. Rather, we attempt to deal only with those complexes of facts which are amenable to historical method. We ask only those questions which the method can answer. We internalize the method's questions and permit a self-censorship of the questions intrinsic to our lives. Puffy with pretensions to "pure scholarship," this blinkered approach fails to be scholarly enough, precisely because it refuses to examine so much that is essential to understanding the intention of the text and our interest in reading it.

Preoccupation with technique leads to a self-perpetuating reductionist spiral. Existing technique determines the direction of further inquiry, including the developing of additional techniques, which themselves presuppose the previous techniques, *ad infinitum.* In this process there is no room for an examination of premises, nor is there any capacity to question the appropriateness of the techniques employed for answering the questions which the text might pose.

Technologism need not be disastrous, whether in oil production or in biblical criticism. But it must be subordinated—always, in every field, without exception—to an adequate hermeneutic. Yet, in spite of remarkable strides in hermeneutical thought, biblical technologism reigns unchecked. The horse rides the horseman and the goal is not reached.

4. Biblical criticism became cut off from any community for whose life its results might be significant.

Historical biblical research, as long as it was situated in an antithetical position to orthodoxy, was the *Wehrmacht* of the liberal church. During this period its relationship to the vital centers of an entire community's life was crucial. Gradually, as success became assured, a shift took place. The community of reference and accountability became, not the liberal church, but the guild of biblical scholars. The guild, however, is not a community but a collective. It is simply a peer group on the model of any other professional guild, subject to the same virtues (preservation of high standards, rewards in terms of prestige to those deemed most worthy, centralization and dissemination of information, etc.) and vices (development of an "expert" ethos, invention of a technical esoteric language, repression of innovation, conformity to peer-group values) which characterize all other professional groups.

This removal of scholarship from a vital community had consequences disastrous for both. For the community it was disastrous because its own self-consciousness as a people under the Word was largely deprived of critical and constructive contributions. For scholarship it was disastrous because the questions asked of the texts were seldom ones on which human lives hinged, but those most likely to win a hearing from the guild. Historical criticism sought to free itself from the community in order to pursue its work untrammeled by censorship and interference. With that hard-won freedom it also won isolation from any conceivable significance. For since truth is not absolute, but only approximate and relational, its relevance can only emerge in the particularity of a given community's struggles for integrity and freedom.

Here the crisis in biblical studies links up with the crisis in the churches generally, since they themselves have become problematic as the locus of Christian community. For many liberal Protestant scholars in America, the most urgent question has become that of finding a context in which their interpretations of the Bible might have significance—or, stated more fundamentally, a context which would give that interpretation significance. Here, as at every other point, the crisis in biblical scholarship is seen as an epiphenomenon of a far more comprehensive crisis in the culture itself.

5. Biblical criticism developed in a historical context which has now changed. In the present context it is, as now practiced, obsolete.

Far too little attention has been paid to the polemical/apologetical origins of biblical criticism. It was first used as a weapon against existing orthodoxies, and only later was it pressed into more constructive service. One of its first exponents, Richard Simon (d. 1712), a Roman Catholic, used historical criticism to undermine Protestant dependency on the Bible as the sole source of authority. Reimarus used it to assault the historical basis of Christianity itself.

The effect was traumatic. Conservative exegesis had interpreted Scripture in the context of a total theological construction of history. The new analytical approach, on the other hand, broke down every total construction in order to arrive at smaller units which might then be recombined through the category of causality. There can be little quarrel that the historical significance of the Graf-Wellhausen hypothesis (which no one today accepts as then formulated) was its usefulness as a method for destroying the conservative view of biblical origins and inspiration, thereby destroying its entire ideology.

As long as this ideological onslaught was made for the sake of desirable fundamental change, that is, as long as it was seeking breathing room for the spirit and the right of the intellect to free inquiry, its thrust was utopian in the best sense of the term: it sought to destroy an existent state of reality for the sake of one which it conceived to be better. Today, however, that war is largely over, and biblical critical scholarship has become the established status quo. Now the unconscious ideological elements in its position have become visible. And the unhappy consequence of this unmasking is not just that liberal biblical scholarship also proves to have been ideological, but that it has ceased to be utopian, and no longer moves toward a greater comprehension of truth. It is as if, at the moment of its victory, it had forgotten why it had fought, and settled down on the field of battle to inventory its weapons in hope of discovering some clue as to their further usefulness. Here, as in other revolutions, those who were fit to overthrow were not fit to govern.

The conservative ideology, for its part, was not wholly deceived by the ideology of objectivism, though it was at a loss to know how to overcome it. For it sensed instinctively that the modernist was not nearly so interested in being changed by his reading of the Bible, as in changing the way that the Bible was read in order to conform it to the modern spirit. Conservatism was not, for all that, juxtaposing a "biblical spirit" to the "modern spirit," but was instead trying to forestall the final dissolution of the precritical spirit of orthodox Christendom. One can today more sympathetically appreciate conservative and fundamentalist anxiety at the loss of religious naïveté. But Christianity needed and still needs the acid bath of criticism. In this case scientific criticism performed an iconoclastic function for faith. If we are today moving toward a "postcritical" epoch, it can only be in the literal sense of the term: *after* criticism, not *above* it! The task now is to find a way forward to what Paul Ricoeur calls "a second naïveté," in which faith performs an iconoclastic function in respect to criticism.[6]

It is in this polemic/apologetic context that the role of "New Testament Introduction" can be understood. "Introduction" was not so much an introduction to the Bible as to the biblical critical ethos. Students studied the great textbooks—Moffatt, McNeile, Enslin—but seldom read the biblical text. "Introduction" provoked an inferno of debate. People's lives changed as a result of its study. Is it any accident that the victory of biblical criticism coincided with a sharp shift of emphasis away from "Introduction" to that of biblical theology—that is, from assault to construction? I have even heard professors wonder aloud why they ever devoted so much attention to introductory problems. There was also, to be sure, the excitement of discovery, the need to press questions to their limits and to establish a certain consensus. Except for certain outstanding problems (including the periodic reopening of issues believed closed), that work is now a part of the history of the discipline, and was a necessary and vital contribution. All that, however, does nothing to mitigate the fact that the questions asked operated at the level of objectivization rather than self-reflective understanding. Introduction served to distance rather than to mediate the text.

The biblical theology movement for its part marked a massive defection from the objectivist paradigm. That it was unable completely to free itself from that paradigm is no judgment on its value. In every revolution the thesis lives on in the antithesis for a time. What Brevard Childs chronicles as the crisis of biblical theology[7] is in fact its desperate opportunity to take the next step forward to a total paradigm change. For we have also learned to do objectivistic biblical theology! We can describe Paul's view of grace with as much benign condescension as we adjudge the carbon date of a Qumran fragment. Whatever the excesses of the biblical theology movement, there is only one that counts, and that is its excessive dependence on objectivism.

Bluntly stated, biblical criticism was a certain type of evangelism seeking a certain type of conversion. No depreciation is intended by those terms, loaded as they are. Only those still under the illusion that biblical criticism was ideologically neutral should be offended by their use. Far more fundamentally than revivalism, biblical criticism shook, shattered, and reconstituted generation after generation of students, and became their point of entrée into the "modern world." The failure of historians of missions and evangelism to register the spectacular evangelistic success of biblical criticism is nothing less than phenomenal, and is but one more indication of the blinding power of its objectivist ideology.

To say that biblical criticism has now, like revivalism, become bankrupt is simply to summarize the entire discussion to this point. It was based on an inadequate method, married to a false objectivism, subjected to uncontrolled technologism, separated from a vital community, and has outlived its usefulness as presently practiced. Whether or not it has any future at all depends on its adaptability to a radically altered situation.

2

Is Biblical Study Undergoing a Paradigm Shift?

In a period when it has become all too stylish to speak of the "death" of the old ways, it is necessary to stress once more that we are declaring a bankruptcy, not holding a wake. It is because biblical criticism has so much of value which must be preserved that it is urgent that it come under new management. What is happening in our field is not essentially different from what other disciplines have already passed through, and it should be of some profit to us to examine their experience. In his brilliant study, *The Structure of Scientific Revolutions*, T. S. Kuhn has traced the process through which scientific paradigms undergo transformation.[8]

Normal research, says Kuhn, is only made possible by a "paradigm"—a constellation of presuppositions, beliefs, values, and techniques which provides a perspective on and a means to manipulate data. Paradigms reduce the chaos of data to a selective pattern which enables specialized research on small pieces of the puzzle. Apart from the paradigm, fact-gathering and observation would be random and diffuse. All seeing depends on a paradigm. No one has ever developed any observational language able to report anything but what is at least generally known in advance, that is, what the paradigm has prepared us to see.

Conversely, however, the paradigm helps us not to see data which it judges to be irrelevant or immaterial. The paradigm suggests which investigations might prove worthwhile and is able to predict results.

Each proposed new paradigm has encountered sharp resistance at the beginning. After it has become established, "normal science" takes over, and mopping-up operations generally occupy the whole careers of researchers. Novelty is not only not sought under normal circumstances, but is strenuously resisted, since its presence, unresolved, would indicate the breakdown of the paradigm. Novelty is forced into the conceptual boxes supplied by the paradigm; if it refuses to submit, the paradigm is in crisis.

Paradigms provide not just methods, however, but a whole perspective on reality. Consequently, quite often when novelty or anomaly appears, it is at first not even *seen*. Kuhn cites as an example a remarkable experiment in which subjects who were shown anomalous cards (a red six of spades, for example) interspersed in a normal deck, simply could not *see* the card as anomalous (perhaps you even failed to *read* the parenthetical example as anomalous), and sought to subsume it under a known category, even though in doing so they experienced acute discomfort (pp. 62ff.). It is this practiced incapacity to see (due to familiarity with the old paradigm) which accounts for the fact that historically it has been younger researchers in a field or people in adjacent fields who have first recognized anomaly for what it is and taken it seriously. But only the person who knows *with precision* what he or she should expect is able to recognize that something has gone wrong. Anomaly only appears, therefore, against the backdrop provided by the paradigm.

The emergence of new paradigms is generally preceded by a period of pronounced professional insecurity, as the volume and complexity of research increase far more rapidly than its importance or return. This period of acute crisis usually lasts no more than a decade or two, during which time sclerotic positions soften and new openness to competing points of view emerges. The search for assumptions is one effective way to weaken the grip of the old paradigm on the mind and to suggest the basis of a new one. In time it becomes clear that the traditional rules no longer define a playable game.

The application to biblical studies can be made approximately, if inexactly. The paradigm for biblical research has been the historical critical method. The anomaly on which it has now foundered is the inability of that method to render the Bible's own content and intent accessible for human development today. This anomaly has long been sensed (Kähler), sometimes transcended (Schlatter, Barth, Bultmann, to name but a few), but generally disregarded. Today it can be ignored no longer. For what a few saw earlier has now forced itself on common consciousness, the evidence of which is a general malaise and a crisis of morale in the field. The arguments in the first part of this paper constitute the theoretical basis for the position that the historical critical paradigm for biblical study is now obsolete. The task ahead is the development of new alternatives.

3

Toward a New Paradigm
for Biblical Study

By way of one such attempt at a new paradigm for
biblical studies, I propose a dialectical hermeneutic
whose dynamic moments might be schematically outlined
as follows:

1. Fusion
   N^1 Negation of fusion through suspicion of the object
2. Distance
   N^2 Negation of the negation through suspicion of the
   subject
3. Communion

This dialectic would apply both to the exegesis of texts
and to the history of interpretation as a whole.[9]

Between the naïveté of uncritical fusion with the horizon
of one's own heritage and the sundering of that unity by
the distance of objectification lies a moment of negativity
which can be variously described as suspicion, alienation,
doubt, detachment, temptation, or death. And between this
alienated distance and the birth of communion lies a negation of the negation, a recoil of suspicion against the sus-
pector, an analysis of the analyzer. This second negation
opens the way to an interaction between reader and text

that can make possible our own personal and social development today.

1. Fusion

In the beginning is the stream of tradition in which we live and move. At least for Western culture, however secular, there can be no reading of the Bible which is not already predisposed by a certain way of seeing, by key ideational preconceptions and preliminary intentions (*why* we read this text and not another) which are themselves a function of the influence of the biblical tradition. The tradition is our world, prior to all "objectivity," all conceptualizing, prior also to our own subjectivity.[10] It is so encompassing, so close as to escape notice. We see right through it; yet we can see nothing without it, since it provides the grid of meanings by which we filter the manifold of experience. It is our horizon. The idea of "the past" is already an objectification. But at the level of fusion, the past is the present of the heritage as the matrix in which we perceive our existence. Tradition furnishes us with our conceptions, it hides itself in our language, it provides the "available believable" which sets the parameters of belief, and it provides an orientation for the process of reasoning.

N¹: Negating the Fusion

First fusion, then confusion. A suspicion is planted. A doubt festers. One dares to question the tradition, to think the unthinkable. This is the first negativity, the achievement of distance from the heritage by means of its objectification.

> The experience of truth, as simultaneous exposure of untruth, includes an element of negation . . . the capacity for truth presupposes the capacity to negate, and . . . only a being that can entertain negativity, that can say "no," can entertain truth. And since the power of negation is a part of freedom, indeed a defining ingredient of it, the proposition

is that freedom is a prerequisite of truth . . . the negation first operative in the experience of truth is defensive
rather than offensive: it is concerned to parry a thrust of
the world, not to harry its reserve. . . . If so, the truth-event
has at first the character of un-deceiving (oneself), and
only much later also that of "un-concealing" or "unveiling" (the veiled things: the latter is Heidegger's formula for
the initial meaning of truth). . . . It is the suggestiveness, the
persuasive likenesses, the manifold make-believe of things
as *perceived* that we are prey to, long before we are plagued
by their secretiveness and our curiosity: they too "talk" to
us in many tongues, and time and again are found out to
have "lied" by "pretending" to be what they are not. . . .
[Then we seek to penetrate] "behind" appearance–to a truth
different from it in kind. Then truth as *by nature* hidden
confronts appearance that by nature hides it.[11]

Negation is here an essential objectification and hence
distancing of oneself from prevailing cultural and intrapsychic images and preunderstandings, and consequently
a dialectical moment of necessary alienation on the way to
freedom and truth. Negation requires an initial suspension
of prevailing understandings–"a flight from knowledge
that is to be cured by knowledge."[12]

This objectification is, by nature, a phenomenological reduction of the life-world in order to open the world
with all its structures to view as a phenomenon which can
be analyzed. Such analysis yields distinctions like those
between subject and object, fact and interpretation. An
essential characteristic of historical existence is precisely
the *absence* of such distinctions. It is hard even to speak
adequately of their interlacement, so tangled are they in
ordinary experience. Of necessity, however, the scholar
objectifies experience; he abstracts a certain "core" from
the complexity and concreteness of an event. This process
of abstraction of "facts" by means of "objectification" provides him with a point of view for comparing other points

of view and proposing functional connections of his own. If he lacked these reference points, his work would be rendered a purely descriptive recital. Phenomenological reduction is thus a necessary device in loosening the threads of the fabric of experience.[13]

The term *reduction* is significant. Its use derives from metallurgy. The image is one of smelting an ore in order to "reduce" it to the desired mineral. What we call "reductionism" then is actually a *failure* of reduction—too small a fire, not enough heat, and the consequent loss of valuable metal. In theology this failure has usually been described spatially—a reductionism fails to include in its explanation certain "higher elements" (metallurgy again!) of human experience.[14] In all fairness the image could be inverted, for theology has failed to include in its explanations "lower" elements of experience (sexuality, family relations, human psychological development), which is equally reductionist.[15]

The Bible, wrenched from its matrix in ecclesiastical tradition, is thus objectified by critical scholarship. It was, to be sure, written by persons, but it can no longer be treated as an immediate Thou, since it has passed into the world of objects by virtue of the act of writing. It is the objectification of the thoughts, experiences, emotions, and visions of persons, but an object nonetheless. As such it has rights which the scholar attempts to champion, both apart from the tradition which enshrined it, and apart from his own enmeshment with it or bias against it. A special *askesis* is laid upon the analyst. He must seek to disentangle his and his culture's history from the text before him. He must attempt to withdraw his projections, overcome his defenses, achieve sympathetic penetration of the text in its otherness, and restore genuine distance through interpretation. It is this "otherness" in its fascination and mystery which requires protection against subjectivism, propagandistic exploitation, projected self-understandings, and all the other ways we generally fail to hear and see the other in its otherness.

Consequently, though objectivism has been exposed as a false consciousness, *objectivity* cannot be surrendered as a goal. It is more than just a special word for honesty, for what is at stake is an elementary respect for the other and its rights.

So the scholar distances the Bible from the church, from the history of theology, from creed and dogma, and seeks to hear it on its own terms. In this search he is sometimes aided by his tools, the "criticisms." They were well named: for source, form, and historical criticism not only prepared the ground for interpretation; they also provided the initial negativity required for distantiation. The knowing which knows it knows not is not immediately possible with a text ingested from childhood or perceived as an alien cultural superego. The "criticisms" serve the function then of decomposing the "picture" of Jesus and the early church delivered by Christendom. It is only after the negation of the ecclesiastical and intrapsychic images of Jesus and primitive Christianity that we ourselves are thrown into the open space where genuine questioning, and hence freedom and truth, becomes possible.

Such a view of "freedom" and "truth," however, is admittedly Faustian, and already from the outset antitraditional. *Behind the apparent neutrality of objectification is the movement toward liberation implied in negation.* Distantiation is not simply, as Heidegger puts it, letting being speak. It is a way of telling it to *shut up*, until we can sort out some of its many voices. The subject, remarks Jonas, "gains by losing but loses nevertheless" as a result of screening out the overstimulation of data in order to reduce it to an abstract image, that is, in order to see at all. Sight is the ideal distance-sense, the only sense in which the advantage lies not in proximity but in distance. "The best view is by no means the closest view . . . we consciously stand back and create distance in order to look at the world, i.e., at objects as parts of the world: and also to be unembarrassed by the closeness of that which we wish *only* to see;

to have the full liberty of our scanning attention." Only, this distance can put the observed object outside the sphere of possible relationship or environmental relevance. In that case, perceptual distance may turn into mental distance, and the phenomenon of disinterested beholding may emerge[16]—what I have called alienated distance.

Not only does the subject lose by gaining; the object loses too. The very terminology, *subject* and *object*, has an independent power quotient in grammar, where *subject* connotes activity and *object* passivity (note the verbal form *to subject*!), with the suggestion of the division of reality between animate and inanimate, agents and things, beholder and beheld.[17] Thus the text's speaking is disallowed from the outset, all our protestations about a "theology of the Word" to the contrary.

2. Distance

The goal of a genuine objectivity is thus in actual practice undermined by a will to power structured into the very semantics of language and expressed through a mastery of the object through technique. We presuppose the present as correct, normative, absolute, then suspend it because the past cannot "compete" on our terms, and then try to "appreciate" the past "in its own terms," thus abandoning the question of its truth.[18]

This association of knowledge with ego-enhancement and power over the world and people is, as we suggested, Faustian. Faust's knowledge by itself, however, is not working for him. He begins to despair. He has studied philosophy, jurisprudence, medicine,

and even, alas, Theology
all through and through with ardour keen!
Here now I stand, poor fool, and see
I'm just as wise as formerly.[19]

His despair is the breach in fusion, the seed of negation. But he is unable to proceed alone. He bargains with the Devil for a bit of distance.

It is no accident that Satan appears just at this point in Faust's disquietude, just in the midst of a critical exegesis of the opening verse of the Gospel of John. For in the phenomenon of critical distance lies the psychogenesis of the image of Satan. All that is peculiarly satanic stems from Satan's refusal to remain with the other angels and his urge to establish himself as one independent being. The final goal of Satan is to become master of the entire world. Such mastery is possible, however, only by the repression of knowledge of the world's true "Father" (Rom. 1:18-32!). Thus the image of Satan aptly illustrates both the Oedipal relation, at the level of personal development, and the subject-object dichotomy, at the level of world-perception. He who would master the world without relation to its ground and origin thus plays the Devil.[20]

Objectification can thus be seen as a special form of the problem of "fallen consciousness," of which Satan is the archetypical representation. Objectification is the consequence of an independence which is out of communion with its own ground: an alienated consciousness.

The process of repression has its analogue in objective research, in the process by which we select out data: the individual separates what will be forgotten from what will be remembered and separates himself from aspects of both in the very act of discrimination. Lost from sight to him is the ideological character of this procedure, with its operational amnesia concerning the shaken and problematic nature of his own existence.

Satan has an Oedipus complex. His neuroticism includes self-protection, self-assertion, and self-expansion; the formation of separations, isolation, alienation, aloneness; the repression of thought, feeling, and impulse. Bakan calls this constellation of alienated consciousness *agentic knowledge.*[21]

Nevertheless, Bakan sees something inherently therapeutic in the Devil and in demonic energies. For in the myth of Genesis 3, God is set on perpetuating fusion by holding man unconscious. The Devil, on the contrary, is the counterforce which renders man conscious, through disobedience. An alliance of the ego with the Devil is necessary to make it possible to achieve the requisite distance which would allow for the development of authentic selfhood.[22] Paradoxically, selfhood is only achievable by fall and loss; the way up is the way down. But this very process can prove the Devil's undoing, for by permitting successful distance to be achieved, by bringing the demonic into the light, the demonic is stripped of its demonic (i.e., unconsciously compulsive) character. "The Devil's very permissiveness is the cause of his own destruction."[23]

Biblical criticism can now be seen as just such a "diabolical" rebellion against the reigning superego of dogmatic Christendom. In liberal Protestant circles, that rebellion has largely succeeded. Distance, and consequently the possibility of freedom and truth, was won. For a time biblical criticism played a creative role in genuine liberation and individuation, insofar as its "agentic" function was dialectically related to what Bakan calls "the communion function," that is, the process by which separation is finally overcome.

Today, however, biblical criticism is the new Establishment. Now, not dogmatic Christendom, but the biblical guild functions as the harsh superego in the self of many exegetes. Insofar as a person submits to its standards in order to receive approval, recognition, and advancement, there is effected an "internal transference" of the ego to the superego. One's own intrinsic powers, life-questions, and deepest yearnings are sacrificed in the interest of acceptance by "them"—thus placing the justifying authority of the self outside the self in such a way that, regardless of the rewards, only anxiety can result. In his schematism of the "natural history of Satanism," Bakan speaks of this self-defeating anxiety syndrome as "denial"; in classical theology it is better known as "bondage of the will."[24]

It is essential that the dual character of distantiation be kept clearly in mind. Satan is an ambivalent, not a purely demonic, figure. He carries the existential truth of a necessary evil which each person recapitulates in his separation from a fused identity with his parents and from his belongingness to his heritage. This ambivalence attached to biblical criticism. On the one hand, it played a central cultural role in deconversion to an anti-creedal analytical attitude. In doing so it uncovered (and continues to uncover) invaluable information for which we should be eternally grateful. But simultaneously, it suffered a gigantic inflation concerning its own reconstructive powers in the life of the spirit. In fact it was incapable by itself of reconstruction, because its very life was methodological skepticism, which is destructured in principle. As a compensation for the anxiety created by the breakup of the tradition, what actually developed was a tendency either to bifurcate existence and preserve one's piety in isolation from the searing winds of criticism, or else to live *through* the negation by living *off* the negation.[25] The second alternative has become increasingly dominant. Objectivism is precisely this attempt to live off the negation by enshrining the subject-object dichotomy as normative for all existence and then seeking to find one's life through the mastery of objects. If the first alternative is an illusion, the second is idolatry.

It is not a theologian, but a psychologist, David Bakan, who dusts off that last term. Idolatry, he believes, is a loss of the sense of search, of the sense of the freshness of experience. It is overquick fixing upon any method or device or concept as the ultimate fulfillment of the life-impulse. Idolatry is "allowing the impulse to be bribed by incomplete but immediate satisfaction." As in neurosis, idolatry is to become arrested at a way station, usually for the small satisfaction that is to be had at that stage. Instead of reacting vividly to actual stimuli, in response to their specific nature, we react repeatedly with rigid patterns provided by our given methodology. "My definition of idolatry conceives it as a kind of 'being stuck'." This being stuck he dubs "methodolatry," the worship of method. "When there is a worship of these methods themselves rather than the objective toward which they are directed, then indeed does science become idolatrous."[26]

The judgment on biblical criticism is not, then, that it doesn't work, but that it has "got stuck" in the second moment of the dialectic of understanding. It has become fixed and immobile in the antithesis, rigidified in a necessary but alienated distance, and captive in its very victory. Unable to extricate itself from its own diabolical descent, objectivism must itself be negated to be transcended.

N²: Negating the Negation

One always wanted to respect fully the distance of the interpreter from the text, but for the same reason one wanted also to overcome it.[27]

There can be for us no retreat from analysis, no flinching from the knife of criticism. However future ages may judge us, it has become our destiny to follow this way to its end. But that end is dialectical, not linear. Criticism rounds upon the critic. There is a further work of destruction, but this time a destruction of what destroys, a deconstruction of the assurances of modern man. There is another kind of suspicion, but this time a suspicion lodged against ourselves, against those who suspect what is suspected.[28]

Do not forget that, as Marx once said, the educator himself has to be educated; in modern jargon, the brain of the brainwasher has itself been washed. The historian, before he begins to write history, is the product of history. . . . It is not merely the events that are in flux. The historian himself is in flux.[29]

This requires that we put ourselves at a distance as a first step in overcoming the alienated distance of objectivism.

"To object": this is the counterattack of the object against the manipulative self-assertion of the subject. The object by objection can, for its dialectical moment of ascendency, subject the subject long enough to listen. This restores the true meaning of "object": *objectum*, something thrown in the way (from *jacere*, to throw, and *ob*, before). It becomes *Gegenstand*, not *Objekt*; that which stands over against us as resistance, opposition, and tension, as opposed to the passive recipient of a scrutinizing, active subject.

The greatness of Freud, says Bakan, lay not simply in his astounding facility for maximizing distance with respect to modes of thought in which minimal distance prevailed initially—things like dreams, slips of speech, or jokes. Rather, it was his enormous courage in the willingness to make, not just his own and his patients' dreams, *but his responses to them*, the subject of investigation. The result was a public psychoanalysis, one which relieved his own depression and opened the way to a new kind of therapy.[30]

What Freud achieved, biblical criticism has, on the whole, failed to do, remaining frozen in a distance that provides not a perspective for relating, but rather remoteness from view. We have failed not only to penetrate the object in communion with it; we have failed to be in communion with our own selves and to allow penetration of ourselves by the object. If objectification is the necessary flight from union wherein the subject renders itself invisible to analysis and hence invulnerable in respect to the object, then it is precisely at the point of subject-vulnerability that a way forward can be forged.

The psychotherapeutic relationship is suggestive of a different relation between the reader and the text. For the healing relationship must be at once objective, in order to provide the distance to see, and personal, so that transference may come about. Even more, the analyst must be willing to change. Carl Rogers stresses the very real risk involved in psychotherapy. For

> courage is required. If you really understand another person in this way, if you are willing to enter his private world and see the way life appears to him, without any attempts to make evaluative judgments, you run the risk of being changed yourself. You might see it his way, you might find yourself influenced in your attitudes or your personality. This risk of being changed is one of the most frightening prospects most of us can face. If I enter, as fully as I am able, into the private world of a neurotic or psychotic individual, isn't there a risk that I might become lost in that world? . . . The great majority of us could not *listen*; we would find ourselves compelled to *evaluate*, because listening would seem too dangerous. So the first requirement is courage, and we do not always have it.[31]

Respondeo etsi mutabor: I respond though I must change—this is Rosenstock-Huessy's answer to Descartes. Cartesianism gave man distance from nature in order to catch the questions flung by it, to ponder the answers, and to make them known. But that way of answering has now become a social problem itself.[32]

Interpretation must now pass through a second negativity: the loss of our own emotional predisposition not to be unsettled, our easy acquiescence to contemporary questions, languages, and perspectives. We must pass through a fiery river of social and self-analysis in order to make possible what Ricoeur calls "an archaeology of the subject."[33] This archaeology is aided by two approaches: a sociology-of-knowledge analysis of the cultural role of biblical criticism and a psychoanalytically informed critique of the way we read the text.

A. A Sociology-of-Knowledge Approach

In the vast sweep of secularization, biblical criticism played an essential role vis-à-vis the demystification of the religious tradition. Jürgen Habermas has described the way secularism deprived traditional world views of their power as the unifying mythic consciousness and centering ritual of a culture. On the one hand, insofar as traditional beliefs could be "useful" to secular ends (i.e., the rise of capitalism), they were reshaped into a supportive religious ideology (i.e., the Protestant ethic). On the other hand, insofar as the religious heritage remained an impediment to secularism, it was relativized by critical analyses which demolished it brick by board down to the historical foundations of belief, reconstructing it as a new edifice on quite different foundations: rationalist ethics, historical causation, the principle of analogy, disbelief in miracle, etc. What was thought to have been given from the heart of eternity is now seen as a human construct, filled with foibles and tainted everywhere by man. If anonymous scribes, not Moses, wrote the Pentateuch, and Jesus never spoke the Sermon on the Mount as we now have it, who is to be believed? The scholars, of course! The authority of tradition passes into the hands of the critics of tradition.

By this careful reconstruction the tradition *seems* to be retained, and demolition passes as renovation. Yet nothing is the same. Under the guise of scientific objectivity and antiseptic disinterestedness, the legitimating authority of traditional belief has been seized and bent to the service of new legitimations by a new authority. By claiming a scientific character this new world view has been able for several centuries to disguise its ideological nature. An ideology, by definition, compels suspension of doubt about the legitimacy of its claim to validity. Thus the ideology of secularism was born, replacing traditional legitimations of power by appearing in the mantle of science and by deriving its justification from the critique of tradition, *thereby keeping actual power relations inaccessible to analysis and to public consciousness.*[34]

It might be instructive to compare the role that biblical criticism played in the demystification of the Bible with that of the Kinsey reports in the demystification of sex. Both depended on their approximation to scientific models for their persuasive power and authority. Both purported only to be descriptive, and maintained an objectivist stance; but in fact neither was value-neutral. Both led to the creation of a new "world" of perspectives, changed values and actions. Were the changes that resulted simply the consequence of letting people know the truth? This is the claim made. But just as no one could conceive and prepare the Kinsey questionnaire *unless sex was already from the outset demystified*, so no one would even consider using the analytic historical method unless the demystification of the Bible was presupposed from the start. Nor will I hide behind a value-free analysis of these developments. Demystification is essential to secularization, and a necessary step in clearing a space for genuine human freedom. Only, it is no great blow for freedom to accomplish this demystification under the guise of a new mystification, or to present a new path to *freedom* under the banner of a presumed scientific *necessity*. (Consider also the *formative* effect of public opinion polls.) In this way "pure description" masks a commitment to a certain kind of cultural transformation, thus "keeping actual power relations inaccessible to analysis and to public consciousness."[35]

The clearest example of how little biblical criticism has been value-free is provided by Morton Smith in a statement which is exceptional only for its candor, not its convictions. Historical criticism, he says, is "atheistic" in the classical meaning of the term. That is to say, if there are gods, they do not intervene in the world's affairs.

It is precisely this denial which is fundamental to any sound historical method. . . . But the historian does require a world in which these normal phenomena are not interfered with by arbitrary and *ad hoc* divine interventions to produce abnormal events with special historical consequences. This is not a matter of personal preference, but of professional necessity, for the historian's task, as I said at the beginning, is to calculate the most probable explanation of the preserved evidence. Now the minds of the gods are inscrutable and their actions, consequently, incalculable. Therefore, unless the possibility of their special intervention be ruled out, there can be no calculation of most probable causes—there would always be an unknown probability that a deity might have intervened.[36]

Few practicing biblical scholars would take exception to this, even those who speak of God's acts in history, since these are generally viewed as mediated through the selfhood of human agents. So acclimated are we to this attitude of functional, methodological atheism that we may no longer be shocked by the vast gulf between this view and the Bible's, where God is depicted as directly intervening in nature and history at will! From the outset, therefore, the biblical scholar is committed to a secularist perspective. If he wishes to discover meaning in the texts at all, he has but three choices: he may attempt to interpret the text by a program of demythologization; he may opt for a practicing atheism, whereby references to God in the text are in every case reducible to another explanation; or he may delude himself into believing that there is no hermeneutical problem.

Now we have a vantage point from which to view the split consciousness of the "believing" biblical scholar. On the one hand, he studies the Bible because it witnesses to the reality of God, and because he wants to let that reality be effective in his personal and corporate life. On the other hand, he must study as a functional atheist. The method itself alienates him from his very objective. It establishes a gulf which can never be bridged as long as he is frozen in distance. It is the Faustian complex: bondage of the will.

If alienation from the objective ("faith," "God," "truth") were the sum total of mischief done, the issue could easily enough be resolved by opting for unbelief. But this alienation is the twin of another: our own alienation, in the act of scholarship, from ourselves.

> Modern theory is about objects lower than man; even stars, being common things, are lower than man. . . . [Even in human sciences, whose object *is* man,] their object too is "lower than man". . . . For a scientific theory of him to be possible, man, including his habits of valuation, has to be taken as determined by causal laws, as an instance and part of nature. The scientist does take him so—but not himself while he assumes and exercises his freedom of inquiry and his openness to reason, evidence, and truth. Thus man-the-knower apprehends man-*qua*-lower-than-himself and in doing so achieves knowledge of man-*qua*-lower-than-man, since all scientific theory is of things lower than man-the-knower. It is on that condition that they can be subjected to "theory," hence to control, hence to use. Then man-lower-than-man explained by the human sciences—man reified—can by the instructions of these sciences be controlled (even "engineered") and thus used. . . . And as the use of what is lower-than-man can only be for what is lower and not for what is higher in the user himself, the knower and user becomes in such use, if made all-inclusive, himself lower than man. And all-inclusive it becomes when it extends over the being of one's fellow men and swallows up the island-kingdom of the person. Inevitably the manipulator comes to see himself in the same light as those his theory has made manipulable; and in the self-inclusive solidarity with the general human lowliness amidst the splendor of human power his charity is but self-compassion and that tolerance that springs from self-contempt: we are all poor puppets and cannot help being what we are.[37]

Thus there arises a perspective in which the development of a discipline *seems* to be determined by the logic of scientific-technological progress. The quest for knowledge becomes itself a function of necessity and retains this aspect throughout its career, which is a continuous response to the new necessities created by its very progress. "The skill possesses its possessor."[38] This technocratic compulsion, which sets up a sense of necessity in the development of method (recall Morton Smith's "professional necessity"), becomes, in Habermas's terms, a background ideology which takes upon itself legitimating power. It has become the singular achievement of this ideology to detach society's self-understanding from the frame of reference of relational, reciprocal, communicative *interaction*, with all of its symbolic reinforcements, and to replace it with a scientific, objectivist model which aspires to the self-reification of men under categories of manipulative rational action and adaptive behavior. "For the first time man can not only, as *homo faber*, completely objectify himself and confront his achievements that have taken on independent life in his products; he can in addition, as *homo fabricates*, be integrated into his technical apparatus."[39] The final triumph of the ideological power of the technocratic consciousness is the obliteration of the difference between controlling and relating, between manipulation and communion, not only from the consciousness of the sciences but from men themselves.

The attempt at mastery of objects leads to the loss of the master. In evacuating his selfhood in order to disappear from view as the objective observer, the viewing subject forgets the magic words that can restore his materiality. Like the ancient dybbuk separated from its body and consigned to wander the world, modern man senses his detachment from life as the peculiar curse of his modernity, the price paid to Satan in return for distance.

Let me illustrate the consequences of objectivist alienation by means of the parable of the Pharisee and the tax collector (Luke 18:9-14).

He also told this parable to some who trusted in themselves that they were righteous and despised others: "Two men

> went up into the temple to pray, one a Pharisee and the
> other a tax collector. The Pharisee stood and prayed thus
> with himself, 'God, I thank thee that I am not like other
> men, extortioners, unjust, adulterers, or even like this tax
> collector. I fast twice a week, I give tithes of all that I get.'
> But the tax collector, standing far off, would not even lift
> up his eyes to heaven, but beat his breast, saying, 'God, be
> merciful to me, a sinner.' I tell you, this man went down
> to his house justified rather than the other; for everyone
> who exalts himself will be humbled, but he who humbles
> himself will be exalted."

The parable is simple and clear: God passes over the "ill-righteously indignant" Pharisee, who presumes himself so superior to the sinful publican, in favor of the one willing to call his own life into question. The parable is almost a mirror of the hermeneutical situation, but our interest in it lies elsewhere.

The scholar's task in exegesis is obviously to explicate the social roles of the two figures, explain that the hearers would at first identify with the Pharisee as the bearer of religious and social status, and then suffer shock and consternation at the wholly unexpected justification of the publican. The scholar, having finished his work, lays down his pen, oblivious to the way in which he has *falsified the text* in accordance with unconscious tendencies, so much so that he has maimed its original intent until it has actually turned into its opposite. For any *modern* reader at all familiar with the text knows that (1) "Pharisees" are hypocrites and (2) Jesus praises the publican. The unreflective tendency of every reader is to identify with the more positive figures in an account. Consequently, modern readers will almost invariably identify with the *publican*. By this inversion of identification, the paradox of the justification of the *ungodly* is lost and the social implications for the reader ignored. What the *story* teaches is the transcendence of *both* role typifications in the "third" perspective of Jesus.

For it is Jesus who declares the publican justified and not
the man himself, since the publican has accepted and internalized the judgment of religion over him ("a sinner"). The
last verse (14a) articulates not what the tax collector says,
but what he was precisely unable to say. To enter the space
in which this parable speaks requires that we hold Pharisee
and publican together as dual aspects of a single alienating structure, represented here by the temple; to locate
both kinds of responses within our own experience; and
to transcend both by their reconciliation under the justifying love of God. But to *begin* by identifying with the
publican as if he were the "good guy" is simply to flip the
righteous/unrighteous tag. The story is then deformed into
teaching cheap grace for rapacious toll collectors. All this
because the exegete hid behind his descriptive task without examining the recoil of the parable upon contemporary
self-understanding. I know of no more powerful way to
underline the inadequacy of a simply descriptive or phenomenological approach which fails to enter into a phe-
nomenology of the *exegete*.[40]

Or again, Christian scholars have tended to identify with
Paul in his attack on the god-man Christology of his Corin-
thian opponents, without sensing the vast gulf between
Paul's situation and our own. Paul himself may have at
one time embraced a *theos aner* view, only to break with it
later as a result of its inherent tendencies toward divisive-
ness and overweaning pride. In any case he boasts that
he "spoke in tongues more than you all," performed signs
and wonders proper to an apostle, and had ecstatic visions
(1 Cor. 14:18; 2 Cor. 12:12; 12:1-5). The early church was
itself born of a dramatic inrush of power and Holy Spirit. It
was in just this context that the Pauline cross-kerygma had
its relevance and bite. It was intended to check (not kill)
enthusiasm and to restrain those whose egos had become
overinflated, by placing them under a nonlegal but real
constraint. We reconstruct the scene, side with Paul, and
treat his position as normative for dogmatics. But we stand

in quite a different spot. Apart from the charismatic movement, our communities are scarcely threatened by an inundation of power, enthusiasm, or ecstasy. Quite the opposite! When we take over Paul's theology of the cross without exegeting our context, this theology, originally conceived as a means of harnessing power for the sake of others, becomes a rationalization of our powerlessness, our spiritlessness—the jaded, enervated religious malaise of twilight Christendom.

One last example must suffice. There is in Revelation 18 (again following the lead of Mottu[41]) an *implicit social critique* which can be analyzed under the Marxist categories of religion as distress and protest.[42] Latent in the liturgical form of this passage there is a primitive or "savage" political analysis of the Roman Empire. As such it is suggestive of a theology of liberation. But that raises the question of who can read and appropriate such a text, since it is addressed not to the carefree scions of privilege, but to those who, like the early Christians, are in some manner oppressed and who, at the same time, under the impulse of *ressentiment*, wish to free themselves from prevailing injustice.

It is no accident that historical critical commentaries on this chapter have generally failed to register any awareness of the consequences of a serious reading of this text for today. Indeed, the biblical interpreter who is satisfied with the existing order of things is only too likely to set up the chance situation of the moment as absolute and eternal, and to conform the text to his situation so as to minimize its power to unsettle his self-understanding and lifestyle. Here we can suspect, in ourselves and others, an infiltration of the social position of the investigator into the results (including omissions!) of his study. We read the text with a whole constellation of commitments, class attitudes, economic and career anxieties, defense mechanisms, and rationalizations, all of which are able to blind us to the contradictions in our own manner of living. Our way of reading must therefore be examined for its implicit ideological bias and blindness. Our liberation from social determination depends upon the degree of insight we gain into the ways *we* are determined, and the conjunction of the otherness of the text with a sociology-of-knowledge analysis of our responses to the text can aid in that process.

B. A Psychoanalytical Approach

The "archaeology of the subject" leads to deeper strata, more personal than social, and for which psychoanalytic tools are more appropriate. For the problem of cultural distance is not only a matter of conceptual and linguistic *difference*. It is also, as Paul Ricoeur reminds us, a problem of *forgetfulness* of the radical questions enshrined in the language and conceptions of another time. Forgetfulness, however, is nothing other than what psychoanalysis means by selective repression. Now if interpretation is, as Gadamer says, the attempt to hear again the question which occasioned the answer provided by the text, then forgetfulness of the perennial questions of existence is a major block to interpretation.

This is an insight long ago recognized by the rabbis. They had a tradition to the effect that the oral law was given in its entirety to Moses, but that most of it was soon forgotten. What survives in the written law represents only hints and fragments. According to one version, during the period of mourning for Moses, no less than three thousand Mosaic oral traditions deriving from Sinai were lost. Others were forgotten by Joshua. Many of the exegetical proofs were also forgotten. Some were restored by Othniel's dialectics. Others were restored by Rabbi Akiba.[43] Besides the manifest intent of providing a rationalization for the exegetical program of the rabbinic scholars, this tradition also reflects awareness of the problem of forgetfulness of those very questions and their answers on which full human life depends, and the continual need, by means of exegesis, to seek their recovery for contemporary life. That is why the text is studied at all, as Ernest Fuchs comments. It tells us something that, without it, could no longer be ascertained.[44]

It is necessary then to struggle against our own forgetfulness of the question in the text, that is, to struggle against our own alienation from what operates in the question. This too, says Ricoeur, is a destruction, a deconstruction of the assurances of the destroyer. There is, he argues, a profound unity between destroying and interpreting; any modern hermeneutic must be a struggle against idols, and consequently it is destructive. In the language of the three great "masters of suspicion," it must be a critique of ideologies (Marx), a critique of all flights and evasions into otherworldliness or illusion (Nietzsche), a struggle against repression (Freud). "For what we wish is to hear through this destruction a more original and primal word, i.e., to let a language speak which though addressed to us we no longer hear."[45]

This more primal hearing cannot, however, be achieved by means of demythologizing alone. For there is a certain arrogance in making *our* world view normative for a demythologizing of the ancient world view. We have to struggle against the presuppositions of our own culture, against the assurances of modern man himself, in order to regain that "interval of interrogation" of which Ricoeur speaks, wherein the primal question can once again address us as the question of our own being. This limits demythologizing to the task of differentiating the *etiological* from the *symbolic* functions of myth. By exposing the scientific pretentions of the myth, demythologizing liberates its symbolic function. This permits a "second naïveté," a postcritical equivalent to precritical fusion, a return to the powerful immediacy of symbols—but all this on the basis of distance, on the basis of criticism and "demythologization."[46]

This recovery of the symbolic function requires that the thinking subject be "humiliated": that he abdicate his superior vantage point, given in the very semantics of the subject-object dichotomy. The image of Faust yields to that of Narcissus, confounded by his own reflection. It is the thinking-feeling subject, the *cogito*, and not just the object, the religious symbol, which must now undergo deeper exploration, in order that it can become open to the reality expressed in symbols. For this, Ricoeur proposes psychoanalytic psychology as an "antiphenomenology," the purpose of which is to conduct an archaeology of the subject as a means of reflection on symbols.

And because the activity of interpretation bears a reciprocal relation to the subject's *personal* history, the symbol gives rise not only to thought but to becoming, to individualism, to the metamorphosis of personality.

> The interpreter as he moves from symbolism to rationality will find that he must make another movement, back into the shadows of his ego and history, for he discovers that his being is mirrored in the reality of life and history and simultaneously created by him in the moment of comprehension.[47]

Let me illustrate how such an "archaeology of the subject" might look when carried out in reference to the story of the healing of the paralytic (Matt. 9:1-8; Mark 2:1-12; Luke 5:17-26). The procedure I am about to detail is one actually developed and in use by Dr. Elizabeth Howes and the Guild for Psychological Studies in San Francisco. The material reproduced is a conflation of several different seminars on the same text, drawn both from those in which I participated at the Guild for Psychological Studies and from my own classes. It is offered as a concrete example of at least one way in which the dialectical hermeneutic under discussion is being practically implemented.

Suppose a group of us is in a circle examining the story of the paralytic in a Gospel synopsis, using as our *modus operandi* a consistently maintained Socratic dialogue. Our leader guides us into the text by means of a carefully conceived series of questions, based on his or her own previous exegesis of the text.[48]

First we analyze the passage, noting the differences and seeking to account for them.[49]

The initial line of questioning might run like this:

Q.—How does Matthew's account differ from that in Mark? In Luke? How would you account for the absence in Matthew of reference to the four men, the tearing out of the roof, and the lowering of the paralytic? Why does Matthew not explain the charge of blasphemy? How does the ending of Matthew's account differ from the other accounts, and why? Which appears to be the earlier source?

Q.—What is the form of this narrative? What happens when you remove Mark 2:6-10? Would the scribes have responded the way "all" are said to do in verse 12 of Mark? How do you account for the presence of two discrete forms of the oral tradition (a healing story and a conflict story) in a single narrative? Has the church fused these, or are they expressions of a complex event? What light is thrown on this question by the distant cousin of this account in John 5:1ff.? Or by the similar complex forms in Mark 3:1-6; Luke 13:10-17; 14:1-6?

This line of critical questioning can of course go on indefinitely, to issues of context (the relation of Mark 2:1-12 to the conflict block, 2:1–3:6 and its prehistory), redaction, historicity, and so on. The leader must decide how far to pursue each line of questioning in terms of the available time, his own assessment of the value of the yield in terms of his careful preparation of the text, and the nature of the group's objectives. The issue is not whether we do justice to each question we can conceive of asking, but which questions require the greatest weight in the light of the specific exegetical task.

Rather than blending the Gospels into an undifferentiated harmony, we are able by means of this critical foray to see the actual differences between them. Our results are, however, less than conclusive. Is this account the fusion of

Matt. 9:1-8	Mark 2:1-12	Luke 5:17-26
[1]And getting into a boat he crossed over and came to his own city.	[1]And when he returned to Capernaum after some days, it was reported that he was at home. [2]And many were gathered together, so that there was no longer room for them, not even about the door; and he was preaching the word to them.	[17]On one of those days, as he was teaching, there were Pharisees and teachers of the law sitting by, who had come from every village of Galilee and Judea and from Jerusalem; and the power of the Lord was with him to heal.
[2]And behold, they brought to him a paralytic, lying on his bed;	[3]And they came, bringing to him a paralytic carried by four men.	[18]And behold, men were bringing on a bed a man who was paralyzed, and they sought to bring him in and lay him before Jesus;
	[4]And when they could not get near him because of the crowd, they removed the roof above him; and when they had made an opening, they let down the pallet on which the paralytic lay.	[19]but finding no way to bring him in, because of the crowd, they went up to the roof and let him down with his bed through the tiles into the midst before Jesus.
and when Jesus saw their faith he said to the paralytic, "Take heart, my son; your sins are forgiven." [3]And behold, some of the scribes said to themselves, "This man is blaspheming."	[5]And when Jesus saw their faith, he said to the paralytic, "My son, your sins are forgiven." [6]Now some of the scribes were sitting there, questioning in their hearts, [7]"Why does this man speak thus? It is blasphemy! Who can forgive sins but God alone?" [8]And immediately Jesus, perceiving in his spirit that they thus questioned within themselves, said to them, "Why do you question thus in your hearts?	[20]And when he saw their faith he said, "Men, your sins are forgiven you." [21]And the scribes and the Pharisees began to question, saying, "Who is this that speaks blasphemies? Who can forgive sins but God only?" [22]When Jesus perceived their questionings, he answered them, "Why do you question in your hearts?
[4]But Jesus, knowing their thoughts, said, "Why do you think evil in your hearts? [5]For which is easier, to say, 'Your sins are forgiven,' or to say, 'Rise and walk'? [6]But that you may know that the Son of man has authority on earth to forgive sins"—he then said to the paralytic— "Rise, take up your bed and go home." [7]And he rose and went home. [8]When the crowds saw it, they were afraid, and they glorified God, who had given such authority to men.	[9]Which is easier, to say to the paralytic, 'Your sins are forgiven,' or to say, 'Rise, take up your pallet and walk'? [10]But that you may know that the Son of man has authority on earth to forgive sins"—he said to the paralytic—[11]"I say to you, rise, take up your pallet and go home." [12]And he rose, and immediately took up the pallet and went out before them all; so that they were all amazed and glorified God, saying, "We never saw anything like this!"	[23]Which is easier, to say, 'Your sins are forgiven you,' or to say, 'Rise and walk'? [24]But that you may know that the Son of man has authority on earth to forgive sins"—he said to the man who was paralyzed—"I say to you, rise, take up your bed and go home." [25]And immediately he rose before them, and took up that on which he lay, and went home, glorifying God. [26]And amazement seized them all, and they glorified God and were filled with awe, saying, "We have seen strange things today."

a miracle story with a conflict story? If so, which if either is historical? Or is it, like three other healing-conflict stories and its distant parallel in John, a mixed form, reflecting perhaps a complex *event*? I am no longer confident that we can decide definitely either way. In situations like this, when the critical conclusions are ambiguous (as is so often the case), scholars tend to become dogmatic in order to defend the critical method. As a result, evidence is sometimes presented with more assurance than is warranted; what begins as a possibility becomes in the next paragraph a probability and ends as indisputable fact.

It just may be, however, that the critical *procedure* is more important than its results. By means of it we have achieved distance. It has undermined residual or manifest views of plenary inspiration, literalism, and bibliolatry, and has set the conditions for a pre-Christological and non-sanctimonious reading of the life of Jesus. In doing so we have brought to the fore the literary problems. It is not always necessary to solve them before going further. It may not even be necessary to dwell at any great length on critical prolegomena. In each pericope the problems of the text itself, and not the critical method, should determine the manner in which techniques are employed.

Now we seek to enter more deeply into the story, each person proceeding on the basis of those critical conclusions which commend themselves as most cogent. (It is a dogmatic fallacy to demand a consensus where matters of probability are concerned.) Working through the account once more, we now try by means of historical imagination to revivify the scene so far as we are able, with historical and literary data serving as continual checks on speculation.[50] This intermediate step enables us to ask what Jesus or the church understood to be the relationship between healing and forgiveness, what was meant by "the Son of Man," or what is presupposed in the pericope about the nature of God. Such factual questioning avoids premature self-reflection unchallenged by what is most alien or unexpected in the text.

This second line of questioning might include questions such as these:

Q.—Try now to picture this scene as it is described in Mark. For what purpose do the four friends bring the paralytic to Jesus? What do they do when they can't reach Jesus? What did Jesus "see" which he identifies as "faith"? What evidence is there as to the attitude of the paralytic himself? Why does Jesus speak of forgiveness? Does Jesus forgive him? How do the scribes hear him?[51] What is meant by "which is easier"? Who is the Son of Man?

Once again, a third time, we take a fresh look at the text. Only this time the distance collapses upon us in an interrogation of the subject. It becomes necessary to ask how the text resonates in us. The insight that revolutionized the analysis of dreams—that the characters in the dream represent psychic phenomena within the dreamer—has a certain applicability to the analysis of other texts as well. For even if, unlike a dream, I did not produce the story in the text, its capacity for evocation depends on its resonance with psychic and sociological realities within or impinging upon me. It is therefore legitimate to introject the characters in the Gospel story as probes into one's own self-understanding.

A third line of questioning might proceed then as follows:

Q.—Who is the "paralytic" in you? That is to say, with what aspect of ourselves does this character resonate, if any? (long pause)

A.—It is the way I've been overacademized. The way I reduce everything to an intellectual exercise.

—It's the suppressed power I have as a woman, which is only allowed expression as bitchiness. Women weren't—aren't—supposed to have strength.

—It's the loss of my whole feeling side, my incapacity as a man to know how I *feel* about things that happen.

—My "paralytic" is a decade of semi-childhood lost. I don't know how to find it again.

—It's my inability to speak up in groups like this.

Q.—Now, who is the "scribe" in you?

A.—It's the part of me which is always judging me, making me feel unworthy.

—My "scribe" is my intellectualism. My theologian. My skeptic.

—The "scribe" in me is saying it doesn't like what you're doing in this discussion.

—It's the part of me that can think well of myself only by repressing all knowledge of the injured, imperfect, or evil parts of me. So it hates me for having a paralytic, and does everything in its power to keep it down.

Q.—But why doesn't the "scribe" want the "paralytic" healed—both in you *and* in the story?

A.—Because he can't admit that this too is a part of him. He wants too badly to think well of himself.

—That's why I'm so self-righteous around people who represent this part of me. I see in them what I can't admit is in me and then try to cut them down.

Q.—So what is the relationship between the "scribe" and the "paralytic"?

A.—Well, the paralytic is as bad off as the scribe, since he's internalized the scribe's judgments of him as being accurate. Isn't that why Jesus has to *begin* by forgiving his sin? The man accepts for himself the current notion that sickness is the result of sin.

—And if this is psychosomatic paralysis, he may be right. At least Jesus treats him as if his guilt is real.

—I think the paralytic wanted to be sick. I mean, if Jesus thinks he needs forgiveness, possibly the guy did do something that has led him to seek punishment unconsciously. And what better way than to be immobilized, incapable of sinning again! So Jesus has to go right to the heart of the matter and see if the man is ready to let his punishment go.

—Yeah, he's playing God, like, he judges and pronounces sentence on himself: You dirty sinner, I'm going to paralyze you for that!

Q.–Okay, this is speculative, but speculation based on what's given in the text and what is known of certain kinds of functional paralysis today. But how are the "paralytic" and "scribe" related?

A.–The paralytic needs the scribe to condemn him. The scribe needs the paralytic to feel superior to.

–So every "scribe" has his "paralytic," and every "paralytic" has his "scribe"!

Q.–Now, who are these four helpers? What resources are available to bring us to the healing value? What would it be like to marshal your paralytic and helpers to move to the healing source? That, after all, is what the story's about, isn't it?

A.–Do you mean inner or outer?

Q.–How would you answer that?

A.–I'd say both.

–I just wonder if I have four friends who would do this for me.

–In any case we don't heal ourselves. This isn't "self-actualization," but participation in a process which leads to healing.

–I'm getting really angry about the way this discussion is going. I feel as if we've just fallen back into the old trap of talking about it as if it were just a matter of understanding and straightening ourselves out, of self-therapy, or even group therapy. I've been down that road, and that's not where I'm at. For me the issue is forgiveness. Does forgiveness really happen, and do we know what it means actually to be forgiven? I mean, are we just going to sit around parading our hang-ups, or does God have something to do with all this? (long pause)

–Yes, why does Jesus use the "divine passive" ("Your sins are forgiven" as equivalent to "God forgives your sins")? Is he saying that God forgives his sin, or simply, look buddy, forget your guilt-trip, it's all over, like the whole sin thing is a big hang-up and Jesus doesn't buy it?

—I think that's a modernization. I think Jesus took sin seriously, but God more seriously still.

—Jesus was fighting for this cat's life. He's saying, right, you sinned, but here's a new start. The power that gave you life says, "Start over, you're all right, I love you. Now take off."

—Let me see if I can say what I'm feeling. The *scribes* think Jesus is claiming to forgive sins. *Jesus* may or may not be claiming that power—there's a tension between "Your sins are forgiven" and "The Son of Man has authority on earth to forgive sins"—but he is clearly *asserting* the man's forgiveness. The *church* certainly believed Jesus was forgiving his sins—at least in Matthew's conclusion: "They glorified God, who had given such authority to men." Could you say it this way: The healing power had its locus in Jesus. But it also had its locus in the paralytic. And Jesus could evoke that power in the man. And this same power continued to have its locus in the church.

—You're talking about the Holy Spirit.

Q.—Could you say that without using "Holy Spirit"?

A.—(After some discussion the group agreed on the following as the content of the phrase "Holy Spirit"): Jesus evoked the life-transformative process in the paralytic.

—That's why he had to come to Jesus. Someone has to spark it in you. If we could do it for ourselves, we would.

—But the man also had to do something. He not only had to come, but to trust Jesus when he was told to take up his bed and walk.

—Is that what is meant by the Son of Man here? Is that merely a title of Jesus, or does it refer to an immanent principle of eschatological wholeness in each of us? Is God transcendent God immanent in the Son of Man?

(The period ends. Each participant is given a bag of clay and asked to model their "paralytic" or their "scribe" in the light of the day's discussion and bring it to the next seminar.)

In this example we still employed the critical tools (source, form, redaction, historical criticism). Have we then contradicted what was said at the beginning about the bankruptcy of biblical criticism? Not at all. For these "tools" are now under new management. After every scientific revolution, as Kuhn points out, while the researcher still uses much of the language and methods he used before, he does so to different ends and within a different gestalt.[52] It is most certainly *not* a question of serially adding to the old techniques and tools new ones, such as sociology and psychology. That can take place under the old paradigm (and has!) without so much as touching the problem of objectivism. The issue from the outset has not been the need for new and better tools, but the solution of the fundamental anomaly of the field: the failure of the old paradigm so to interpret Scripture as to enable personal and social transformation today. The techniques and the "agentic" manner of thought employed by the historical critical method were themselves functions of the kinds of questions asked and the presuppositions shared under the old paradigm.

Theory and practice are therefore not so simply disentwined. In a certain sense the historical critical paradigm has been, like Paul's notion of the Law, our pedagogue till now. A new paradigm means both the supercession and the fulfillment of the old. It is necessary to assert this, on the one hand, against those who would incorporate the new within the old and, on the other, against any historical critical Marcionites who, out of justifiable frustration or simple sloth, are ready to throw over the old altogether. When we take up previous methods into a new totality we are not then "beginning with the Spirit and ending with the flesh." After all, it was precisely those who said that Christ was the end of the Law who ransacked the Old Testament like a treasure trove! So let me repeat: the new paradigm is a theory and a practice, indeed, a theory about a practice. As such it is constitutive of the entire ethos connected with that practice. To change a paradigm is thus to change theory, practice, *and* ethos. That the scholarship of the future will continue to need critical tools is indisputable; but which and how and in what measure—that is a genuinely open question.

It should be clear from the example that exegesis has been transposed into a holistic context in which questions of technique have been subordinated to the overarching purpose of enabling transformation. It should be equally clear, however, that such self-exploratory analysis is not subjectivism or intrapsychic reductionism, for the understanding of ourselves which the text evokes makes possible a far more profound understanding *of what the text itself actually says.*

This concern for the rights of the text and the deepest possible understanding of it characterizes the approach of Dr. Howes and her associates. To the critical insights and the questioning method of her New Testament mentor, Henry Burton Sharman, Howes has added symbolic analysis and psychological insights drawn from her training under Fritz Kunkel and Carl G. Jung. Building painstakingly over three decades, she and her psychotherapeutic colleagues have constructed an approach to human individuation in which the teaching and deeds of Jesus, plus other biblical material and the mythologies of many cultures, are treated as guides to personal and social growth as an integral part of a world encompassing life-process. Rigorous use of biblical criticism prevents psychologizing and allegorizing, insofar as the attempt is made to recover what Jesus actually taught and how the church in fact interpreted his teaching, and only then to inquire into its psycho-social and symbolic meaning, both for Jesus and the church, and for us today. The net result is the most promising new approach which I have yet encountered. Predictably, as Kuhn would lead us to expect, it originates outside the biblical "Establishment."[53]

Communal exegesis of this sort overcomes the "expert ethos" of professional scholarship, since each person is the primary resource for how the text resonates in her or him. At the same time, the deprivatized, corporate context cures the solipsism of scholarly practice. The interpreter needs the mediation of the felt responses of others in order to discover how he or she is affected by the text's address. Here also a recovery of the revelatory function of art becomes crucial. Through the medium of clay, paints, written dialogue, music, movement, silence, or role-playing, the echo of a feeling, which gives birth to an insight and is evoked by resonance with the text, can be given further body and substance. Insight and feeling coalesce in a story we are striving to tell. When it *becomes* our story—that is, when feeling and insight merge in the symbolic matrix of our being—then the insight furthers the self-formative process.

The insights thus evoked are a rich blend of ancient and contemporary wisdom, of recovered questions and our own existential responses. The problem, however, is not simply that of discovering insights; we must also integrate them into our self-understanding, modifying our thought and behavior by means of their intervention.[54] *For an insight never strikes us as really true or truly real until it can be related to those symbols which most profoundly inform our lives.* All the more powerful then are insights whose very genesis lies in those religious texts which have throughout human history provided the symbolic landmarks for life's orientation.

The insights we seek by means of the text are thus neither general religious or theological truths, nor simply the author's original insights, but the truth of our own personal and social being as it is laid bare by dialectical interpretation of the text. Corporate, Socratic dialogue enables the participants to uncover the ways in which they have mutilated and distorted both the written text and the text of their own experience, and to liberate the depth symbols of existence from a mode of expression deformed as a private language (as neurosis and religion) into the mode of expression of public communion (as community and faith). "The Socratic secret," wrote Kierkegaard, "which must be preserved in Christianity unless the latter is to be an infinite backward step, and which in Christianity receives an intensification, by means of a more profound inwardness which makes it infinite, is that the movement of the spirit is inward, that the truth is the subject's transformation in himself."[55] The spiral of questioning between the text and ourselves moves deeper and deeper, both more inward *and more cosmic*, as one after another link with present experience is forged. What began as destruction and negativity issues in communion.

3. Communion

Everything said earlier about the bankruptcy of biblical scholarship can now be summarized in a single phrase: it "got stuck" in the Faustian moment of alienated distance. The consequence of this separation was objectivism: the subject-object dichotomy. The restoration of communion and genuine dialogue between interpreter and text depends on the practical resolution of the subject-object problem.

A. Subjects and Objects

It has been the argument of this book that one cannot get beyond the subject-object dichotomy except by going through it. In this sense the attempt to eliminate the subject-object dichotomy by an unmediated existential encounter is hopeless. That dichotomy is not only unavoidable; it is *necessary*, in order to fight free from the stream of life which carries us. But it can and must be transcended in a dialectical sense, not by its obliteration, to be sure, but by it transformation. The subject-object *dichotomy* gives way, by means of the archaeology of the subject, to a subject-object *relationship*. Alienated distance is bridged so as to become *relational* distance, in which the integrity of each party is preserved by the reciprocity of dialogue. Subjects and objects remain, each as object of the other, each as subject to the other. Together they become copartners in the quest of life. Having begun (*fusion*) as the object of a subject (the heritage), I revolt (*distance*) and establish myself as a subject with an object (the text), only to find myself in the end (*communion*) as both the subject and object of the text *and* the subject and object of my own self-reflection.[56]

Thus there is achieved a communion of horizons, in which the encounter between the horizon of the transmitted text lights up one's own horizon and leads to self-disclosure and self-understanding, while at the same time one's own horizon lights up lost elements of the text and brings them forward with new relevance for life today. In this encounter some elements of one's own horizon are negated and others affirmed; some elements in the horizon of the text recede and others come forward.[57] Both text and interpreter have been called into question in terms of the answer they have given to the questionableness of existence, which has been given precise form by the text and by our interest in the text. Interpretation is then no longer a question of accepting or rejecting what is said in the text, but of self and social exploration in terms of the question which the text, possibly even in an inadequate or antiquated way, has nevertheless been indispensable in helping us to recover. That is why all knowledge is inevitably linked to the self-formative process of the knowing subject. "In this sense, then, every true hermeneutical experience is a new creation, a new disclosure of being; it stands in a firm relationship to the present, and historically could not have happened before."[58]

Such a conclusion does not imply subjectivism, either as manifested in a will to power over the object or as a projection into the object. On the contrary, it makes possible a genuine objectivity, wherein an interpretation is only able to grasp its object and penetrate it in a relation in which the interpreter reflects on the object and himself *at the same time* as moments of an objective structure that likewise encompasses both and makes them possible.[59]

Paradoxically, we are more certain of the unfathomable depth in ourselves, once it has been revealed to us in experience, both that it is and what it is, than we are of our own consciousness. And we know that the wholeness which we all at heart seek is not under our conscious control (though we must cooperate with it), but lies beyond us as a process to which we can only offer ourselves. This process gives itself to be known by us; it comes before us as subject in the relation of object. It meets us in the great myths and religious texts, preeminently in the figure of Jesus of Nazareth, and shows a knowledge of us which we ourselves lack. As knower I know that in the knowledge gained of the object I am first of all known. There is here an unveiling through the object that discloses to me a depth beyond my reckoning, a depth through which I begin to be released from egocentric stratagems and reunited with all creation.

If the subject-object *relationship* dialectically supplants the subject-object *dichotomy*, and in doing so establishes a communion of horizons, then there is worked a transformation of our life-relation to the text. The interests which motivated our reading, and the applications we hoped to secure, move from the fringe of consciousness to which they were exiled by objectivism, and occupy a place of honor in the full light of critical awareness.

B. Interests and Applications

The Faustian negation was no "disinterested" quest for truth. It was profoundly interested. It sought ruthlessly to clear space for autonomous selfhood by negating heritage. But it was for all that no less a genuine quest for truth. For its pursuit of knowledge was a movement aimed at emancipation. It had a stake in autonomy and responsibility. It only became untrue when it disguised its "emancipatory cognitive interest" (Habermas) from itself and others, and failed to allow truth's recoil against the subject. Only when reason's interest in reason was hidden from the process of reasoning did the dichotomy occur, with the consequent loss of reason's unity with experience and its capacity to enhance individuation.[60]

"The highest interest and the ground for all other interest is interest in ourselves."[61] The issue is not selfishness, which is in fact aborted self-interest incapable of realization. Interest is rather the will to existence, to survival, wholeness, and pleasure. It is thus not as secondary inference from the reasoning process, but is constitutive for all knowing and acting whatever. "Interest precedes knowledge even as it only realizes itself through knowledge." As an act of freedom, interest precedes self-reflection just as it realizes itself in the emancipatory power of "self-reflection."[62]

This unity of reason and the interested employment of reason conflicts with the objectivist concept of knowledge as pure theory untouched by the practical concerns of life. But we have already seen how in fact interests were rendered abstract and surreptitiously projected onto objects. The objectivist finds himself only in the representation of things, dispersed and immersed in objects. Biblical scholars could avoid the hermeneutical question for so long precisely because the scholar, having projected his interest onto the text, could regain it only vicariously through the "objective" restatement of what lay in the text, without any reference to himself or his community. Now, at the end of the procedure, to reintroduce the *real* concerns which initially motivated his research would be to show his hand— as having been in control all along! Hence the results of inquiry were rendered inaccessible to practice. Insofar as he is unable to summon up the courage for self-reflection, the scholar lives in dispersal as a dependent subject that is not only determined by objects but is himself made into a thing.

Once again the psychotherapeutic relationship provides a helpful alternative. For here we meet, not an interest in knowledge for knowledge's sake, but an interest in knowledge as enlightenment which promotes healing in actual persons. Knowledge and interest fuse. "It is not that interest inheres in reason; rather, reason inheres in interest."[63] It is because the patient is sick that reason is enlisted to help him. Suffering and desperation generate an interest in criticizing one's own false consciousness. The dialogue between therapist and patient promotes a relearning process which, impelled by the passion for criticism and the desire to be made whole, reunifies the self that has been internally in conflict. In the therapeutic relationship, then, theory and practice, research and treatment, linguistic analysis and personal experience, coincide. The healing process is in fact synonymous with the uncovering of truths repressed or never known.[64]

Religious texts have had this same quality of urgency. They have aimed at healing or alleviating the wound of existence, of providing a meaning without which life cannot continue. These too are issues of existence and survival, at a level more profound than psychotherapy. Here more than anywhere else, reason and fantasy join hands in the task of imaging and attaining the "good life." The latter, writes Habermas, is neither a convention nor a timeless essence, but the vision of that measure of emancipation that historically appears objectively possible under given yet modifiable conditions. It is in imaging the exact specificity of this vision of the "good life" that reason and fantasy discover their common interest. This is why reason, unless it is ideologically ensnared, inclines toward the progressive, critical-revolutionary, but tentative realization of the major dreams of mankind, and why it can no longer be divorced from the intuitive and feeling functions of the imagination.[65] How did biblical scholarship, whose subject matter is so saturated with eschatological imagery, lose sight of the fact that we have always only studied the past in the name of a desirable future?

For too many of us too much of the time, our emancipatory interest in the text, which originally led us to seek in it the insights that evoke transformation, has been bribed by more superficial interests such as advancement, publication, or fame. These intervening interests are purely "agentic," however, and lack any practical relationship to the truth of the text. In fact, the question of truth is beside the point, for a publication need not be true to bring about public recognition; in some cases quite the contrary.[66] Knowledge is thus separated from experience, theory from practice, reason from the interest in reason, scholar from life-context.

If, on the other hand, our interest is recentered around the depth-concerns of our existence—if, for example, we define our interest as the search for personal and social transformation in the light of the teaching of Jesus—then we already presuppose a process which makes transformation possible. And to seek the question which renders my own existence questionable is to assume that my not yet being what I am is encompassed by the possibility of becoming what I am but am not. When we "let the text speak," therefore, we do not value equally everything it has to say, but fashion an order of ranked priorities in terms of the resonances it establishes with our own unknown but higher potentialities. We know of this unknown through our or the text's unanswered questions. Therefore we do not listen just for what pleases us. Indeed, we learn to watch for what displeases us, what is most alien to us, since our interest is explicitly in being altered.[67] It is because we do not know who we are that we need the text. For the insights which it makes possible are the means by which, in Ricoeur's words, we advance toward our being.

Apart from the *initial* conviction that knowledge is consummated in communion, the dialectic of interpretation does not climax in transcendence but only reversal, in an infinite series of reversals: the antithesis simply becomes a new thesis, which is displaced by a new antithesis, *ad infinitum.* We would not have entertained the first negativity had we not believed that our betrayal of the heritage would lead to higher truth. Why would we have busied ourselves with the very text which the heritage enshrines, unless we believed it taught *another* truth which the heritage had lost?

So we listen to the text. But with whose voice does it speak? It is a text still, not a person. It has no voice of its own. "Letting the text speak" is, after all, only a figure of speech. Whose voice? Bultmann's? Marx's? Jung's? Calvin's? Billy Graham's? The text is *mute*! So apart from the *prior* assumption, from the very outset, that something speaks through the text which called the text *and myself* into being, the text is cast into a swamp of total relativism, and interpretation is reduced to ventriloquy.

So I repeat: in the text I hope to encounter an alien speech which is finally the self-disclosure of God. That is the ultimate ground of the attempt at objectivity. For if I scramble the message, if I impose on the text my own subjectivity, I close off to myself my own transformation, including whatever social consequences hang thereon. There is a "passion of the text," as someone has called it; like a sheep led to the slaughter, it openeth not its mouth. Only *this* mouth is not dumb, but gagged, rendered speechless by our domination. Objectivity is not "disinterestedness," therefore; it seeks to hear the alien speech precisely because it *is* interested, and passionately so, because the very life-formative process of the creation itself is at stake.

Our interest, therefore, implies application. *It is our desire to apply which led us to read*—unless, that is, we are out of relationship with our own existence and seek only to quarry the text for publishable tidbits (but that too is an "application" of sorts). This self-explorative application of the text to our own present for the sake of a desirable future is not, then, the last act of study. It is implicit from the outset.[68]

Not only that, but the text does not disclose its meaning *unless* our world becomes clarified at the same time. One comprehends the substantive content of the tradition only by applying that tradition to oneself and one's situation through an interpretive translation. Application *furthers* the insight; it determines whether or not it was valid, and extends its meaning through contact with lived experience. For meaning at least partly depends on what questions we are asking in the present. Consequently, "understanding the text is always already applying it."[69]

It has seemed to me that the arguments of this book, both negative and positive, have a bearing on the reading of the Bible in any context, or for that matter, the reading of any "eminent text" significant for life, whether it be in history, philosophy, literature, or law. For that reason I have attempted to avoid restricting my comments solely to the role of the Bible in the church. I can avoid doing so no longer, however, for a peculiar characteristic of the Bible itself is its concern to establish a community around that reality to which it bears witness. We saw earlier that the church has been rendered problematical as the locus of Christian community. The American churches are in a cultural Babylonian captivity. But for some reason the captives still want to be free, many of them, and suspect that the Bible might light the way. There are no doubt other contexts in which the Bible can be fruitfully read and studied, new forms of community in which the Bible plays a central role in growth. But in the final analysis the Bible is the church's book. They go to Babylon together, together languish by the River Chebar, together wander home. There are people today who long for liberation. (Scholars are people too.)

All this, of course, spells a certain amount of upheaval in the role of the scholar. On the one hand, research will always be necessary, even as the questions change. And in research the longest way around almost always proves surest. An extended detour, temporarily holding questions of relevance at a distance, plowing in philology, combing through the debris and traces of centuries, leafing through ponderous books—all this tedium and eyestrain may be the most fruitful way to the heart of the matter—*if* we get to the heart of the matter. That approach is not the only way, however. A situation of oppression or need, such as addiction or persecution or personal crisis, can sometimes provide its own spontaneous hermeneutic which simply overleaps the problem of the past. In this case personal suffering or social alienation has already provided distance from normative cultural interpretations (the state of fusion). Either approach has its limitations. Biblical scholars must resist the temptation of establishing themselves as scribal mandarins jealously pocketing the keys of knowledge. And the oppressed and nonexpert must avoid the temptation of anti-intellectualism and that form of "pneumatic exegesis" which simply reads off the text what one already thinks he knows. How much each could learn from the other, if only they could more often be seated around the same table!

Why then should we continue the anachronous practice of making the model of the biblical scholar normative in the training of students? Scholarship is the vocation of only a few for the sake of the many. The model for students should be not the biblical scholar, but the biblical interpreter—a person competent to help any group of people understand the impact of the Bible in human transformation. By binding the interpreter to the needs of real people in everyday life, the tendency to "get stuck" in an alienated distance can be effectively countered. At the same time the interpreter no longer need always defer the actualization of the "word-event" to the preacher. This handy bifurcation of professional "areas" (I research, you preach) is legitimate no longer. For what the spoken word of preaching is able to do (*sometimes*; the "new hermeneutics" often speaks as if it happens automatically every time the preacher opens up his mouth!) is to overcome the objectification of the text which results from its having been written. But this same goal can be achieved in the act of communal exegesis itself, where the text again becomes speech addressed to persons as a word to which each must personally respond. That means that the interpreter need not always confine himself to prolegomena,

but can share in the word-event as contributor and participant. Such communal exegesis will not replace preaching,
but it is on a par with preaching, and, where it is practiced,
serves to renew preaching (and the preacher!).

In the solidarity of our shared interest we come together
around the text. We wish to learn something from it, not
better, but different, something we did not know at all, or
only sensed dimly. *Respondeo etsi mutabor*: we are ready
to listen even if we must change. And in rare moments of
lucidity and courage we may listen *in order to change.*

> In order to arrive at what you do not know
> > You must go by a way which is the way of ignorance.
> In order to possess what you do not possess
> > You must go by the way of dispossession.
> In order to arrive at what you are not
> > you must go through the way in which you are not.
> And what you do not know is the only thing you know.[70]

This kind of knowing is not the quest for certainty about
things known, but the search for the unknown. We no longer regard knowledge as a truncated pyramid in which
each advance in knowledge diminishes the unknown, with
an eye to its final abolition. Such an image of the intellectual quest is nothing more than an egocentric device
for controlling our anxiety about existence. Instead we
perceive knowledge as an inverted pyramid opening out
onto infinity, in which each advance in knowledge leads to
greater wonder and wider vistas of unknowing. The text,
the tradition, the human community, I myself—these are
not problems susceptible of technological manipulation
only (as indeed they are in the moment of agentic distance),
but mysteries requiring unveiling, insight, revelation. Such
knowledge is not mastery but participation received as a
gift. Understanding is substituted for mastery.

The agency of Satan as a dynamic necessity for the
establishment of distance must now be surrendered, for the

ego becomes aware of portions of reality that lie beyond its mastery, the recognition of which deprives the satanic role of its compulsive power. With the surrender of mastery in the ego's sense there comes about a more profound mastery, now no longer premised on repression.[71]

The Faustian notion of freedom as the absence of superego constraints or restrictions from the side of tradition is thus revealed to be bondage of the will in separation from and yet in symbiotic dependence upon the heritage. Freedom as unconstraint is superseded by freedom as the capacity for communion. We are no longer locked in a standoff between the tradition and ourselves. There is instead, in Gadamer's words, a dialogue between the *distanced* tradition and our belongingness to a tradition.[72] In this communion of horizons the dialectic of interpretation attains for a short moment the goal of understanding; then the horizons shift, our self-understanding and world change, we see the past in a different light, and the process begins anew.

> And what there is to conquer
> By strength and submission, has already been discovered
> Once or twice, or several times, by men whom one
>   cannot hope
> To emulate—but there is no competition—
> There is only the fight to recover what has been lost
> And found and lost again and again.[73]

Conclusion

"Woe to you Scholars! for you have taken away
    the key of knowledge;
you did not enter yourselves,
    and you hindered those who were entering."
                        —Luke 11:52

It has been all too easy for us scholars to deceive our-selves about our situation. Even the excitement with which we have greeted each new technique has been due in part to the vain hope that it might solve the field's basic anomaly. Form and redaction criticism, now more recently audience criticism, structuralism, psychohistory, and socio-logical analysis, all of these, if only added serially to the old objectivist paradigm, can do nothing to dislodge us from our alienated distance. If we are bankrupt, it is not because we have not tried, but because we have continued to try too long in the wrong way.

For we are dealing with not simply false notions but an alienating ethos: a principality and power which shapes not only our thoughts, but our lifestyles, self-images, ambitions, commitments and values. No simple shift of categories will touch that. We are possessed, and we require exorcism. We must be freed from dependence on the good opinion of the guild, from anxiety about success as professionally defined, from Faustian perversity which has become frozen in the dialectical moment of distance, from a critical suspicion directed everywhere but at ourselves.

And are there those who say they are not possessed? Very well. But those who know their possession and have fought to become free speak differently. *They* say: no lon-ger possessed.

This essay has been nothing less than an attempt at pub-lic exorcism. Its primary object is myself. It is not directed against any other persons as such, but at a particular role typification which is never, thank God, wholly incarnated, but which, to the degree that it is internalized as the professional superego, exercises demonic compulsive power over the self. Before it our finest hermeneutical and personal convictions are rendered powerless. I have personally found it extremely difficult to admit that I have taken away the key of knowledge. I have sought to hide that fact by the normal display of academic erudition and role dependency. To become free—to "respond though I must change"—for many of us that spells a kind of dying. Indeed, the dialectical hermeneutic proposed here is nothing other than a methodological elaboration of the truth of losing and finding one's life.

> He must unlearn his heroic willing; let him be uplifted as well as exalted—let the other lift him up, devoid of willing!
>
> He overcame monsters, he solved riddles; but now let him absolve and redeem his monsters and riddles and transform them into children of heaven. . . .
>
> To stand with muscles relaxed and will unharnessed is the hardest task of all for you, you exalted men!
>
> I credit you with all the evils; that is why I want the good from you.[74]

We conclude then where the matter belongs: not simply at the level of our professionalism, but of our humanity. It is not simply for the future of a discipline that we struggle, but for our lives. Perhaps it is too much to hope for, but let us hope nevertheless: for a new paradigm—a new, more human way—for biblical study.

Afterword

I am pleased that Walter Wink's *The Bible in Human Transformation* is being republished and pleased to have been invited to write an afterword. Walter and I met more than twenty years ago when we were both actively involved in the Jesus Seminar, and we have been friends ever since, so I will refer to him as Walter in the rest of this afterword.

The first sentence of this small but important book is startling, bold, and memorable. It sounds like the start of a manifesto: "Historical biblical criticism is bankrupt." Like most bold statements, it is an overstatement—but one that contained truth when it was written and still contains truth almost four decades later. Much of biblical scholarship as practiced within the mainstream academy has been concerned only with the "objective" analysis of ancient texts, as if we scholars were curators of a museum of antiquities. But the Bible has transforming power, for individuals, communities, and the world. Our task, in Walter's words from the first chapter of this book, is "so to interpret the Scriptures that the past becomes alive and illumines our present with new possibilities for personal and social transformation."

Quite ironically, given this book's first sentence, Walter has become one of the foremost historical biblical scholars of the last forty years. But he has not succumbed to the scholarly temptation to be a curator of a biblical museum. Instead, his books have been marked by passion—a passion for what the Bible means to those of us who live within communities that seek to be faithful to it and transformed by it. It is a disciplined passion: Walter knows and uses the methods of historical criticism, augmented by his creative integration of insights from other realms of academic inquiry.

Walter's passion for the transforming power of the Bible has flowed into his life. He has lived much of what he writes about. More than most of his colleagues in the academic study of Christian origins, including me, he has lived his life as a Christian intellectual who moves from thought to praxis, by which I mean life- and world-changing action. In workshops around the world, he has trained people in praxis. He has engaged in perilous practice himself, including entering South Africa illegally during the decades of apartheid in order to encourage and equip black South Africans in the methods and goals of nonviolent resistance to oppression—methods and goals grounded in Walter's perception of God as revealed in Jesus.

Though I met him only in the late 1980s, I had known about him since the fall of 1969 when I was in the first year of my doctoral program at Oxford. I had just embarked on three years of reading everything I could about the historical Jesus. I began with Jesus' relationship with John the Baptizer, the mentor of Jesus. I read everything I could find on him, including Walter's 1968 book on John the Baptist, *John the Baptist in the Gospel Tradition* (Cambridge University Press, 1968). I was impressed. Indeed, I regarded him as the world's leading authority on John. Little did I know that he was only about thirty when he wrote the book, just a few years older than I. But he was a "big name" for me, "way back" in 1969.

That was forty years ago. In the decades since, my respect and admiration for Walter and his work have continued to grow. I recommend him and his books to church groups wherever I go (and that's now over a million miles).

I also recommend his books in my own books. I especially recommend *Engaging the Powers: Discernment and Resistance in a World of Domination* (Fortress, 1992) and his more recent small book, *Jesus and Nonviolence: A Third Way* (Facets; Fortress, 2003). Indeed, the latter was one of the textbooks in a course that I taught for many years in a public university. Students loved it—and found it provocative, as Walter's books are.

I have learned much from him, as has the discipline of New Testament scholarship as a whole. Several of his major themes have become widely shared by mainstream scholars. Without trying to be comprehensive, I mention the following notions that have now become part of the "accepted wisdom" of many scholars of the New Testament and early Christianity:

- **The concept and language of "domination systems."** More than anybody else in New Testament studies, Walter has given us language for the most typical form of political and economic organization in the ancient world, and underlined its importance for understanding Jesus and early Christianity. And he makes it clear that domination systems continue in the modern and postmodern world.
- **Walter's understanding of the New Testament language about "the principalities and powers."** This is connected to his emphasis on domination systems, of course, but it deserves separate mention as another of Walter's distinctive contributions he has made. Indeed, he wrote a trilogy (*Naming the Powers* [Fortress, 1984]; *Unmasking the Powers* [Fortress, 1986]; and *Engaging the Powers*) on "the powers" as a crucial element in the early Christian understanding of the world. He then wrote a fourth book (*The Powers That Be: Theology for a New Millennium* [Galilee, 1999]) in which he summarized in one volume his understanding of "the powers that be." He not only highlighted this theme in the New Testament, but has helped to make us aware that "systemic evil" is bigger than any of us as individuals. Whatever we think of the mythological terms in which New Testament language about "the powers" is sometimes cast, the real effects of social and spiritual forces to which that language refers are indisputable. Walter, more than any other New Testament scholar of our generation, has helped us to see this.
- **The claim that Jesus advocated nonviolent *resistance.*** Jesus resisted the domination system of his time and

did so through nonviolent protest and advocacy: protest against oppression, advocacy of a domination-free order brought about through nonviolence. In Walter's exegesis of the familiar sayings in the Sermon on the Mount about loving enemies, turning the other cheek, going the second mile, and giving up your shirt as well as your cloak (Matt. 5:39-44), he argues that these are counsels to and examples of active nonviolent resistance. Moreover, he takes the argument for nonviolence beyond the first century by describing the many times that it has succeeded as a significant means of social change in human history. Thus he counters the common notion that a commitment to nonviolence is unrealistic and argues that it is practical, wise, and right.

Walter is a brilliant New Testament scholar, a valued colleague, a passionate Christian, and a dear friend. It is a privilege to commend to a new generation of readers one of his earliest books, the one in which he first declared his passion for the Bible as a means of God's transforming power.

Marcus Borg
Canon Theologian,
Trinity Episcopal Cathedral,
Portland, Oregon

Appendix

The Work of the Guild
for Psychological Studies

Elizabeth B. Howes, Ph.D. (1973)

The procedure referred to by Dr. Wink on pp. 39ff. has been used by myself and my colleagues in the Guild for Psychological Studies over a period of thirty years. It is based on historical critical study of the New Testament led by Dr. Henry B. Sharman; on the use of the Socratic method of question and discussion; and on enrichment from the insights of religious depth psychology, especially the analytical psychology of C. G. Jung. The sequence in which these elements in our procedure are stated is significant because it places the priorities correctly. The first and central concern has always been the study of the Gospels, pursued with the aim of sorting out as far as possible the life and teachings of Jesus from later Christian accretions. Out of this study and the depths evoked by it, it became evident that more knowledge of the human psyche was necessary. This brought about the inclusion in the procedure of "analytical psychology"— not to "psychologize" Jesus, but to amplify and deepen the profound aspects of his message and the present relevance of his words and actions for individuals and perhaps for the church in its search for revitalization.

The Purpose

The purpose of each seminar is to recover as far as is humanly possible the figure of Jesus from the later Christian accretions, assumptions, and projections on him which are found throughout the Gospels. In this sense the study is indeed "pre-Christological." The concern is to find the religion *of* Jesus in his original stance rather than resting content with the religion *about* Jesus. At every point the tools of critical research are used, and always there is openness and a willingness to acknowledge limitations. But with the use of documentary hypotheses and with the criteria of dissimilarity and consistency, it seems possible to achieve a picture of some accuracy. The purpose of attaining this picture is not based on a prior assumption about Jesus as final authority. It lies rather in the fact that attaining such a picture may enable one to discover that Jesus' personal religion—his relation to God—may offer a way of living that is individually and historically fulfilling. Jesus may disclose some fundamental insight about human nature which is amazingly relevant to what we know today about the psyche or the personality, and he may even more startlingly state lucidly the condition to be met or the process to be followed if one would have "eternal life" or enter the kingdom of God as a state of being here and now. In addition it is altogether refreshing to ask about Jesus' relation to his own inner myth and mythic roots, and his relation to the Christ-image.

Behind all the creeds and dogmas which have over two thousand years grown up around this figure is the figure itself and its reality. Increasingly the emergent struggles in the seminar participants—their desire for individuation, to use Jung's term—led to the inclusion of the understanding of the psyche and the role of symbol. We did not go to the Gospels out of a desire to illustrate individuation. Rather, the central truths of the Gospels needed further psychological illumination for full contemporaneity.

The Method

The procedure we follow is one where the group (usually twenty or twenty-five persons in a circle) reads a passage from a synopsis of the Gospels (we use Henry B. Sharman's *Records of the Life of Jesus*, published in New York by Harper & Row in 1917). The leader then asks questions to which all possible answers may be given by members of the group. It is as if the specific text being studied were put in the middle of the circle and the questions focused in a dynamic fashion in order to help each person to encounter and be encountered by the meaning of the text. The questions are inclusive enough to deal with the problems of biblical criticism, the possible actual outer-historical situations and their meanings, the sociological and religious implications for Jesus' time, the challenge to all members of the group to consider their own socio-political-economic positions, and, finally, the inner deep psychological and spiritual dimension. Optimally each person replies, and each person listens to other replies. More questions are then asked by the leader, based upon both the responses of the participants and the leader's sense of where the discussion is going. In this way a process similar to what Jung calls amplification in dream analysis develops. The symbols and symbolic statements in the text expand and become more meaningful, and each person takes from the text what he or she thinks and feels Jesus perhaps meant. The criterion for leader and participant alike is not "What do I want to think or believe Jesus meant?" but "With all the insights I have, what could he have meant and what could it mean to me?" In this way, all answers are honored. Nothing is labeled "right" or "wrong" except literal misunderstandings. The meaning of the text is thus richly amplified, and out of this process the individual's encounter with the text's significance for him is actualized.

There is no group summary. No consensus is needed. The final point is what each person individually does with his own life on the basis of the confrontation with the material.

The Attitudes Required

The procedure just described has never been easy, for it requires openness about our most basic conceptions and beliefs. The question is not whether these conceptions are valid or not. Rather, it is whether one is prepared to put the search for truth about the person of Jesus as revealed in the Synoptics above cherished beliefs built up during the long history of Christianity. It is often hard to say yes to this search for truth, even though many of the traditional beliefs about Jesus no longer carry religious meaning. For example, Jung points out that the Christ-image has been much too much identified with the side of light, good, and kindness, and is therefore not adequate for the whole self, which also includes elements of darkness. Here it would be relevant to ask what Jesus implied about the nature of the Christ-image and the Son of Man image.

No one can totally cast aside preconceptions, but one can be responsible willingly to participate in such a seminar—to speak, to listen to others, to move always toward greater involvement in the meaning of any passage. This attitude of searching is the only prerequisite for the seminar, and great honesty is required. There will always be resistance to newness, along with excitement. The method also requires the overcoming of egocentricity, which may take the form of wanting to talk too often, feeling that one has the best answer, or never speaking because of the fear that one's ideas "wouldn't be any good."

As regards the leader of such a seminar, he must not only know the material and the critical work to be done on each passage, but also have a living relationship to it that is more than intellectual, or the questions will evoke no response. This requires knowledge of the material and considerable self-knowledge. Thus, as in any other art or science, there is a danger of practicing before one is ripe. Or course the questions will always to some extent reflect the "bias" of the leader, but this can be counteracted in two ways. One such way, genuine although it may seem superficial, is to ask questions which are known to bring out responses contrary to one's own conviction. This is healthy; of course, the leader must constantly be self-aware and self-critical about whether rigidities and dogmatism have crept in. The second and deeper way to counteract bias is for the leader to hold in all humility the conviction that no matter how many times one goes over the material, new insights and dynamisms will come through each time. This occurs because each time the seminar responses are different, depending on the makeup of the group, and because the material itself always contains a mystery which remains unfathomable and numinous.

Some Examples

MATT. 5:21-22a, 23-24; HBS #37a.* ON ANGER.

*Here and following, the "HBS" number given refers to sections in Sharman's *Records of the Life of Jesus*, which I use in seminars as the finest parallel arrangement of the Synoptic Gospels available.

Possible Questions:

What is the contrast between what the Old Testament was saying and what Jesus is saying?

How would you characterize Jesus' attitude toward anger? Is he condemnatory, commending, or what?

What have we been taught about anger? What do we usually do with it?

The anger here is discovered at the altar—what does it mean to be at the altar?

Where, for you, is the altar? What place? What times? What does it symbolize?

What must be going on in us at the altar to let anger rise up?

What is the "gift" to be left during the time of reconciliation, and to be offered later?

What does reconciliation imply?

To whom might the "brother" refer?

Outwardly it could refer to whom, for you? How do we deal with the person if he is open to reconciliation? If he is not?

Inwardly, who might the "brother" be with whom there is anger?

How can we work to come to terms with this part in genuine reconciliation?

How will the work of reconciliation be different, whether outer or inner, because one has been to the altar? What will be the additional value, as opposed to fighting with anger alone?

How will the gift be different after the human work of relationship?

What is the picture you get of Jesus from this teaching?

Problems and Challenges:

There is a dearth of meaning for the idea of the "altar" and of a place and time for prayer or meditation.

Many questions will be raised about reconciliation when the other doesn't respond.

The significance of the realism of Jesus and the wisdom of bringing together religious and psychological insights will be central.

MATT. 11:2-11; LUKE 7:18-28; HBS #41a-e. JOHN AND JESUS.

Possible Questions:

Why does John ask Jesus this question through his disciples? For information, correction, or what? (Recall John's concept in Matt. 3:7-12; HBS #17.)

In vv. 4 and 5, how does Jesus answer?

From where does this quote come?

Compare the original Isaiah passage and its form here. How do you account for the difference?

What is Jesus' answer to John? If it is not a direct yes or no, how would you characterize it?

Put in your own words the sentence in v. 6, "Blessed is he who takes no offense at me."

What is Jesus saying about his relation to the Christ-image? What is your reaction to what you see here?

In vv. 7-9 how does Jesus characterize John? As what kind of man?

In v. 11, what contrast does Jesus go on to make between John as "more than a prophet" and yet not in the kingdom of God? Why is this said of John?

In the light of all we have seen so far of the relation between John and Jesus, consider the following questions: How will the kingdom come? Who brings it in? What must we do personally, beyond "good works"?

Problems and challenges:

Struggle to see Jesus' answer to John's question about the Christ, because it is not a clear yes or no. What further evidence is given here about Jesus' relation to the messianic archetype?

MARK 2:13-17; LUKE 5:27-32; MATT. 9:9-13; HBS #30. ON EATING WITH SINNERS.

Possible Questions:

Describe the scene as you visualize it. Who is present? How are they arranged?

What do the Pharisees criticize Jesus for? Why would they not associate with the "sinners"? What was behind their attitude?

Who would the sinners have been in those days? Who would they be today? What group of people would carry this defiling, contaminating element for you?

What was Jesus' attitude toward the sinners? Why was he able to associate with them?

Take the Pharisee and the sinner who are both inside us. What does the Pharisee represent? Describe him. In addition to seeing the "sinners" outside, when do we also find them inside us—i.e., what part of yourself does the Pharisee most censure or condemn?

Contrasted to the Pharisee-sinner split in those times and in our times, socially and individually, what is the attitude of Jesus? He and the value he represents are closest to which element, the Pharisee or the sinner? What does that really mean? Which has the church been closest to in attitude, the Pharisee or Jesus?

To whom does Jesus refer in v. 17 as "whole"? Which ones think they are "whole"?

Problems and Challenges:

There will be difficulty in facing one's own rigidities and repressed sides.

Keep watching to see whether Jesus will give us a way to face and heal this split.

Notes

1. The Bankruptcy of the Biblical Critical Paradigm

1. Karl Mannheim, *Ideology and Utopia*, trans. Louis Wirth and Edward Shils (New York: Harcourt, Brace & World, 1936), p. 89.

2. Ibid., p. 20.

3. Ibid., p. 122.

4. Ibid., p. 123.

5. R. D. Laing, *The Politics of Experience* (New York: Pantheon Books, 1967), p. 62.

6. *The Symbolism of Evil*, trans. Emerson Buchanan (New York: Harper & Row, 1967), pp. 347ff.

7. *Biblical Theology in Crisis* (Philadelphia: Westminster Press, 1970).

2. Is Biblical Study Undergoing a Paradigm Shift?

8. T. S. Kuhn, *The Structure of Scientific Revolutions*, 2nd ed. (Chicago: University of Chicago Press, 1970).

3. Toward a New Paradigm for Biblical Study

9. By "dialectical" I mean specifically a triadic movement from thesis to antithesis to synthesis. This establishes the schema of fusion, distance, and communion in a dynamic relationship which is tipped off balance forward so as to impel each successive step. For purposes of descriptive clarity such a model is justified. In actual practice, however, work is always more random, more hit-and-miss, trial and error. Historically, dialectic refers to many different forms of argumentation, from dialogue (Socrates, Plato) to disputation (the Scholastics) to a triadic universal process (Hegel). In reference to Hegel's use of dialectic, one should perhaps add that there should be no attempt to read a dialectical movement onto the physical universe, or to install it as a special logic. Nor does the thesis "produce" its antithesis; only our critical attitude does that, and its failure means that no antithesis is forthcoming.

Similarly, "struggle" between thesis and antithesis does not "produce" a synthesis. The struggle is one of human beings, and *they* must produce new ideas. And the synthesis is not just a compromise; it usually contains new ideas which cannot be reduced to earlier stages of the development. Cf. Karl C. Popper, *Conjectures and Refutations* (New York: Basic Books, 1965), pp. 314ff. By dialectic we mean, following Bernard Lonergan, "a combination of the concrete, the dynamic and the contradictory." *Insight* (New York: Philosophical Library, 1957), p. 217; cf. also p. 421.

10. Richard E. Palmer, *Hermeneutics* (Evanston: Northwestern University Press, 1969), pp. 132–33.

11. Hans Jonas, *The Phenomenon of Life* (New York: Harper & Row, 1966), pp. 175–76.

12. Lonergan, *Insight*, p. 200.

13. Larry Shiner, "A Phenomenological Approach to Historical Knowledge," *History and Theory* 8 (1969): 266–74.

14. "I am not bothered by someone who tells me that he is not ashamed of being a reductionist. What does bother me is his failure to perceive that he has not *explained* myths or rituals by being unashamed of reduction." Hans H. Penner, "Myth and Ritual: A Wasteland or a Forest of Symbols?" in James S. Helfer, ed., *On Method in the History of Religions*, Beiheft 8 of *History and Theory* (1968): 52.

15. See Peter Homans's urgent appeal at this point in *Theology after Freud* (Indianapolis: Bobbs-Merrill, 1970), part 1.

16. Jonas, *Phenomenon of Life*, pp. 149–52.

17. James Brown, *Subject and Object in Modern Theology* (London: Student Christian Movement Press, 1955), p. 31.

18. Palmer, *Hermeneutics*, p. 182.

19. Goethe's *Faust*, cited by David Bakan, *The Duality of Human Existence* (Skokie, Ill.: Rand McNally & Co., 1966), p. 67.

20. Cf. Homans, *Theology after Freud*, pp. 141–42. The works of Homans and Bakan have been seminal for my thinking.

21. Bakan, *Duality*, pp. 67ff.

22. "Lucifer was perhaps the one who best understood the divine will struggling to create a world and who carried out that will most faithfully. For, by rebelling against God, he became the active principle of a creation which opposed to God a counterwill of its own." Erich Neumann, *Depth Psychology and a New Ethic* (New York: G. P. Putnam's Sons, 1969), p. 141. This implies, however, that Satan is not dualistically conceived, but images *the*

dark side of God himself, and that monotheism does not mean unity *against* multiplicity but the unity of multiplicity within the Godhead. Rivkah Schärf Kluger, *Satan in the Old Testament*, trans. Hildegard Nagel (Evanston, Ill.: Northwestern University Press, 1967), p. 10.

23. Bakan, *Sigmund Freud and the Jewish Mystical Tradition* (Princeton, N.J.: D. Van Nostrand Co., 1958), pp. 232–33. Cf. also his "Psychological Characteristics of Man Projected in the Image of Satan," *On Method* (San Francisco: Jossey-Bass, 1967), pp. 160–69.

24. Homans, *Theology after Freud*, p. 142.

25. In reference to the former, the biblical theology movement, whenever it flinched from the burden of demythologization, became merely a nostalgia for the past. Devotion to "the Hebraic mentality," schemes of *Heilsgeschichte*, and certain forms of the quest of the historical Jesus leap over the problem of translation by seeking to make a past understanding normative *in its own terms*. There is here a deference to the authority of the past as a substitute for lost union with the present tradition. This requires a projection, albeit positive, of our own life-potential onto an understanding of existence which is not immediately transferable into our mundane lives, and is consequently an illusion, regardless of the historical validity of the reconstruction involved. This amounts to the repression of the consequences of our act of negation, symbolized by Oedipus's blindness. As such it avoids the hermeneutical problem altogether. (It is also, one might add, a frequent error of classicists.)

26. David Bakan, "Idolatry in Religion and Science," in Bakan, *On Method*, pp. 154–58.

27. Ernst Fuchs, "Response to the American Discussion," in *The New Hermeneutic*, ed. James M. Robinson and John B. Cobb Jr. (New York: Harper & Row, 1964), p. 238.

28. Paul Ricoeur, "The Language of Faith"; this and another article to be cited, "The Critique of Religion," were translated by Bradley DeFord in the *Union Seminary Quarterly Review*, Spring 1973.

29. Edward H. Carr, *What Is History?* (New York: Knopf, 1961), pp. 44 and 51.

30. Bakan, *Sigmund Freud*, pp. 232 and 251.

31. Carl Rogers, *On Becoming a Person* (Boston: Houghton Mifflin Co., 1962), p. 333, quoted in Bakan, *Duality*, p. 99. That

psychotherapists often fail to live up to this standard is shockingly documented by the exposé of a patient's "counterattack" against his analytical objectification in "A Psychoanalytical Dialogue with a Commentary by Jean-Paul Sartre," *Ramparts Magazine* 8, no. 4 (October 1969).

32. Eugen Rosenstock-Huessy, "Farewell to Descartes," *Out of Revolution* (New York: William Morrow & Co., 1969), p. 751. The author fails to grasp the continuing dialectical necessity of distance, however.

33. Paul Ricoeur, *Freud and Philosophy*, trans. Denis Savage (New Haven, Conn.: Yale University Press, 1970), pp. 419ff.

34. Habermas, "Technology and Science as Ideology," in *Toward a Rational Society*, trans. J. J. Shapiro (Boston: Beacon Press, 1970), pp. 98–113. Consider, for example, the symbiotic dependency of the biblical critical movement in America on fundamentalism as a source for converts to "deconversion." Criticism requires something to criticize. What then is the future of biblical criticism in colleges and seminaries where students are now arriving *already* deconverted and secularized?

35. "What provokes one to look at all philosophers half suspiciously, half mockingly, is not that one discovers again and again how innocent they are . . . but that they are not honest enough in their work, although they all make a lot of virtuous noise when the problem of truthfulness is touched even remotely. They all pose as if they had discovered and reached their real opinions through the self-development of a cold, pure, divinely unconcerned dialectic (as opposed to the mystics of every rank, who are more honest and doltish—and talk of 'inspiration'); while at bottom it is an assumption, a hunch, indeed a kind of inspiration—*most often a desire of the heart that has been filtered and made abstract*—that they defend with reasons they have sought after the fact. *They are all advocates who resent that name*, and for the most part even wily spokesmen for their prejudices which they baptize 'truths'—and *very* far from having the courage of the conscience that admits this, precisely this, to itself, very far from having the good taste or the courage which also lets this be known, whether to warn an enemy or friend." Nietzsche, *Beyond Good and Evil*, trans. Walter Kaufmann (New York: Random House, Vintage edition, 1966), pp. 12–13; italics mine, except the last.

36. Morton Smith, "Historical Method in the Study of Religion," in Helfer, *On Method in the History of Religions*, p. 12.

Smith does not exclude the possibility of "divine" interventions within the psyche of historical persons. "And even if we supposed (as is probable) that many oracles were not cooked to order, but were expressions of the individual or group unconscious, or of the prophet's 'sincere conviction' . . . even this account of the cause permits, and indeed requires, naturalistic, psychological analysis and explanation. It is a mesh in the coherent web of natural causes and consequences, which a god is not" (p. 13).

37. Jonas, *Phenomenon of Life*, pp. 195–96.

38. Ibid., pp. 193 and 209.

39. Habermas, "Technology and Science as Ideology," pp. 105ff. I leave aside for the time being the no less crucial question of the role played by the historical critical method in justifying the domination of the rising bourgeoisie over the more fundamentalistic working class and over the texts themselves. Henry Mottu asks provocatively in a personal communication whether the bourgeoisie had in fact, under the cover of an "objective" approach, taken for granted that God functions as if He would be on our side. This would explain the ability of the believing scholar to tolerate functional atheism, since the God-question can be left aside because it is answered in advance in favor of the bourgeoisie enterprise.

40. Henry Mottu is engaged in an exegesis of this passage using Sartrian and Marxist categories. This discussion already lies under debt to his developing ideas.

41. From a lecture in a team-taught course at Union Theological Seminary, fall 1970, entitled "Apocalypse and Revolution." The faculty were Paul Lehmann, Henry Mottu, and myself.

42. Cf. Friedrich Engels, "On the History of Early Christianity," in Karl Marx and Friedrich Engels, *Marx and Engels on Religion* (New York: Schocken Books, 1964), pp. 316–47.

43. *Temura* 16a; *Menahot* 29b.

44. Erenest Fuchs, "What Is Interpretation in the Exegesis of the New Testament?" in Fuchs, *Studies of the Historical Jesus*, trans. Andrew Scobie (London: Student Christian Movement Press, 1964), p. 78.

45. Ricoeur, "Language of Faith"; cf. also *The Symbolism of Evil*, trans. Emerson Buchanan (Boston: Beacon Press, 1969), p. 349: "Beyond the desert of criticism, we wish to be called again."

46. Cf. Ricoeur's *Symbolism of Evil*, part 2.

47. Charles H. Long, "Archaism and Hermeneutics," in *The History of Religions*, ed. Joseph M. Kitigawa (Chicago: University

of Chicago Press, 1967), pp. 86–87; cited by Peter Homans, "Psychology and Hermeneutics: Jung's Contribution," *Zygon* 4 (1969): 351ff.

48. The openness of questioning is of course not absolute, as Gadamer points out, since every question already implies the direction in which the answers to *that* question must come if it is to be meaningful and appropriate. With the placing of the question, what is questioned is put in a certain light; it implies an answer. Real questioning then presupposes openness—i.e., the answer is unknown—and at the same time it necessarily specifies boundaries. Everything depends therefore on finding the right questions, which in turn presupposes a continually deepening awareness on the questioner's part. This underlines the importance of listening to the text from the outset, for the text itself is an answer to the question which occasioned it. But questioning means also going outside what is said in the text and encompassing other possible answers. It is inadequate simply to restate the text's answer; the text must be placed within the horizon of the question that called it into being. Hans-Georg Gadamer, *Wahrheit und Methode* (1960), cited by Palmer, *Hermeneutics*, pp. 198–201.

49. The text is taken from *Gospel Parallels*, ed. B. H. Throckmorton (New York: Thomas Nelson & Sons, 1949).

50. This procedure is comparable to the amplification method used in dream analysis, but with contributions from all participants. Cf. Elizabeth Boyden Howes, "Analytic Psychology and the Synoptic Gospels," *Intersection and Beyond* (1971), p. 152; available from the Guild for Psychological Studies, 2230 Divisadero Street, San Francisco, California 94115.

51. Those who regard the account as a compound of two literary units may deal with the scribes at the *redactional* level (asking why the church found it instructive to juxtapose healing with a conflict over forgiveness involving the religious authorities). In either case a claim for experience is being made, whether at the historical or the redactional level: that religiousness can be a social neurosis which blocks the healing of others and oneself, and that its resistance to healing arises from the splitting-off and repression in oneself and in society of what is unacceptable to consciousness (hence the role of forgiveness in the story).

"Scribes" are therefore not simply a kind of Jew, to whom we can, with subtle or blatant anti-Semitism, feel superior. They are endemic to all religions, wherever blame and moral standards are established. Christians almost invariably take a "Pharisaic" attitude toward Pharisees. "Pharisaism," Nietzsche observed, "is not a degeneration in a good man: a good deal of it is rather the condition of all being good." *Beyond Good and Evil*, p. 88.

52. T. S. Kuhn, *The Structure of Scientific Revolutions*, 2nd ed. (Chicago: University of Chicago Press, 1970), pp. 120–35. What changes is not simply the *interpretation* of observations that themselves are fixed once and for all, as many would like to argue. "Rather than being an interpreter, the scientist who embraces a new paradigm is like the man wearing inverting lenses. Confronting the same constellation of objects as before and knowing that he does so, he nevertheless finds them transformed through and through in many of their details. . . . Operations and measurements are paradigm-determined. . . . Scientists with different paradigms engage in different concrete laboratory manipulations. The measurements to be performed on a pendulum are not the ones relevant to a case of constrained fall. . . . After a scientific revolution many old measurements and manipulations become irrelevant and are replaced by others instead. . . . But changes of this sort are never total. . . . Though he may have employed them differently, much of his language and most of his laboratory instruments are still the same as they were before." But even these enduring features have a changed relationship to the ruling paradigm and sometimes even produce different results, as in the celebrated case of Dalton's atomic theory.

53. Since my acquaintance of the Guild for Psychological Studies is somewhat recent, I have asked Dr. Howes to write a brief appendix for this book, outlining the Guild's approach in more precise detail and providing several examples of the kinds of questions asked. For further reference see Elizabeth B. Howes and Sheila Moon, *Man the Choicemaker*, from Westminster Press, Fall 1973.

The urgent task now before us is the development of a variety of such workable models for exegesis in a life-context. See for example the "conversation model" proposed by my colleague J. Louis Martyn, "An Open Letter to the Biblical Guild about Liberation," in a forthcoming Festschrift for Paul S. Minear, edited by Paul Holmer. I am confident there are others of which I need to be informed.

54. "Insights are unwanted, not because they confirm our current viewpoints and behavior, but because they lead to their correction and revision." "They may be accepted as correct, only

to suffer the eclipse that the bias brings about by excluding the relevant further questions. Again, they may be rejected as incorrect, as mere bright ideas without a solid foundation in fact; . . . again, consideration of the contrary insight may not reach the level of reflection and critical consciousness; it may occur only to be brushed aside in an emotional reaction of distaste, pride, dread, horror, revulsion." Lonergan, *Insight*, pp. 191–93.

55. Søren Kierkegaard, *Concluding Unscientific Postscript*, trans. D. F. Swenson (Princeton, N.J.: Princeton University Press, 1941), pp. 37–38. Jürgen Habermas comments on the ontological illusion that Socratic dialogue is possible under any and all circumstances; whereas in fact attempts at dialogue are repeatedly closed off by invisible interests hidden behind objectivism's desire to derive everything from itself. Habermas, *Knowledge and Human Interests*, trans. J. J. Shapiro (Boston: Beacon Press, 1971), pp. 228 and 314–15.

56. "For let this be said now: the subject-object *relation*, which presupposes, holds open, and stands through the duality, is not a lapse but the privilege, burden, and duty of man. Not Plato is responsible for it but the human condition, its limits and nobility under the order of creation. For far from being a deviation from biblical truth, this setting of man over against the sum total of things, his subject-status and the object-status and mutual externality of things themselves, are posited in the very idea of creation and of man's position vis-à-vis nature determined by it: it is the condition of man *meant* in the Bible, imposed by his createdness, to be accepted, acted through. . . . In short, there are degrees of objectification . . . the question is not how to devise an adequate language for theology, but how to keep its necessary inadequacy *transparent* for what is to be indicated by it." Hans Jonas, *Phenomenon of Life*, pp. 258–59; cf. also Schubert Ogden's helpful discussion "Theology and Objectivity," *Journal of Religion* 45 (1965): 175–95; Ian G. Barbour, *Issues in Science and Religion* (Englewood Cliffs, N.J.: Prentice-Hall, 1966), pp. 175–206; and Michael Polanyi, *Personal Knowledge* (Chicago: University of Chicago Press, 1962), chap. 1.

57. Palmer, *Hermeneutics*, p. 244.

58. Ibid. K. M. Baxter, commenting on the relative success or failure of modern playwrights to reconceive a classical play, observes that "this 'shaking up' of a classic demands the power to impose a new pattern on the broken pieces after the jolt has

occurred. This can only be done by someone who is in direct touch with the center from which the original classic was created, someone who can restore concentratedness to them." *Speak What We Feel* (London: SCM Press, 1964), pp. 52–53.

59. Habermas, *Knowledge and Human Interests*, p. 181. The expression "transcending the subject-object relationship" rings like another familiar nostalgia, that of transcending the parent-child relationship. It is not the terms which constitute the relationship as oppressive, however, but rather the *quality of the relatedness*.

60. This entire section lies under heavy debt to Habermas, *Knowledge and Human Interests*, especially pp. 198–213.

61. Ibid., p. 206.

62. Ibid., p. 210.

63. Ibid., p. 287.

64. It is not by accident that we have chosen a personal interaction and developmental model with certain analogies to the psychotherapeutic relationship, rather than the mechanical models of natural science hitherto aped by historiography in its rush for recognition as a science. Naturalistic models have in practice presented a closed scheme of cause and effect wholly autonomous to the investigating agent, whereas the actual process of discovery may lead to a change in the agent in the very act of becoming conscious of meaning. Causal models depend for their cogency on unreflective consciousness; laws are applicable only insofar as people let themselves be determined by them. But self-reflection releases the subject from dependence on hypostasized powers, thus making self-transcendence possible. This is the proper goal of both therapy and interpretation. Habermas, ibid., pp. 256 and 309–10.

Habermas has attempted to extrapolate from the psychoanalytic model to a general theory of knowledge, which he then tests against sociological theory (in his *Toward a Communications Theory of Society* [Boston: Beacon Press]). And in its quiet and unpretentious way the Guild for Psychological Studies has already for several decades been practicing a method of biblical study which achieves the same end for biblical hermeneutics.

65. Habermas, *Knowledge and Human Interests*, pp. 288 and 211–13. See also Homans, *Theology after Freud*, pp. 195ff.

66. Why do trivia like Schonfield's *The Passover Plot* or Allegro's *The Sacred Mushroom and the Cross* find so many fervent readers, while more responsible books languish on the

shelves? Is it not because, as Homans points out (*Theology after Freud*, p. 227), popular culture is a diffuse mythopoetic apparatus thrown into motion by the collapse of the transcendent, one that serves—adequately or not, that is not the point—to "minister" to the nostalgias of the masses? There is, as it were, a will to be disabused, a desire to let nostalgias die. If Christianity can be debunked at its very root, then the painful tug of this nostalgia for the lost innocence of fusion in the ancient tradition can be laid to rest: the ghost of Jesus will grant us peace, if only . . .

Scholars are indignant at the perversion of their art by such publications, oblivious to the fact that their own efforts often serve the same purpose—among the educated elite!

67. The act of desiring an insight "penetrates below the surface to bring forth schematic images that give rise to the insight." When there emerges into consciousness an object coupled with an incongruous affect, then one can investigate association paths, argue from the incongruous to the initial object of the affect, and conclude that this combination of initial object and affect has been inhibited by repression. "For the combination was inhibited, precisely because it was alien." Lonergan, *Insight*, pp. 192-93.

68. So Gadamer, in Palmer, *Hermeneutics*, pp. 235-36. This view of application is poles apart from that implied by the term *contemporization*. Contemporization is itself a problem created by objectivism. It assumes the validity of an undialectical objectification of the past, the detachment of the investigator from the past, and the incapacity of historical criticism to mediate the past to the present (else why a separate effort called contemporization?). One thinks immediately of *The Interpreter's Bible*.

69. Ibid., p. 188. This is true even in the most exact of pure sciences, mathematics. For mathematical theory, as Michael Polanyi observes, can be learned only by practicing its application: its true knowledge lies in our ability to use it. Polanyi, *The Tacit Dimension* (New York: Doubleday, 1966), p. 17. How much more should this be true of the great religious texts, whose sole concern is informing the practice of living?

70. T. S. Eliot, "East Coker," in *Four Quartets* (New York: Harcourt Brace Jovanovich, Inc., 1943), p. 15. Reprinted by permission of the publisher.

71. Bakan, *Duality*, pp. 66-67. With the declining power of the superego to bind impulses, and its replacement in mass culture by behavioral control steered by external stimuli (especially the

mass media), we might hazard to prophesy that the dispropor-
tionate emphasis on the biblical critical tools will also decline.
The ideological, demystifying function of criticism will decrease
even as its essential interpretive function is retained. Not the biblical tradition, but modern secular culture will increasingly be the
heritage from which distance is sought. Here the biblical tradition may actually act as antithesis rather than thesis, and play an
iconoclastic role in reference to secularism (cf. ibid., p. 10). This is
in fact already sometimes the case for students of Scripture who
lack religious roots.

72. In Palmer, *Hermeneutics*, p. 184.

73. T. S. Eliot, "East Coker," p. 17.

Conclusion

74. Nietzsche, "About Exalted Men," in *Thus Spake Zarathus-
tra*, trans. Walter Kaufmann (New York: Viking Press, 1966), pp.
119–20.